CRUMBS &

Create stunning cakes and bakes at home with over 90 recipes from the iconic London bakery

DOILIES

Cupcake Jemma

WELCOME 6

ESSENTIAL KIT 12

ESSENTIAL INGREDIENTS 16

KITCHEN RULES 20

BASICS & BFFS 22

CUPCAKES 70

TRAYBAKES 128

COOKIES 166

CAKES 208

ACKNOWLEDGEMENTS 262

TEAM PHOTOS 264

INDEX 268

WELCOME

Welcome to Crumbs & Doilies! This might be just a recipe book to you right now, but to me it is an extension of our bakery and shop and I'm so happy you're stopping by for something delicious.

———

Maybe this is your first time here. Maybe you've been here a few times and can't stop coming back. Maybe you've been dying to visit for ages and it's finally happening. Either way, I hope you're going to enjoy yourself! You might be at the beginning of your baking journey with only a handful of bakes under your belt, or a frequent baker, who already has some skills and wants to try something new. Whatever your story, you'll find loads in this book for you, from the basics and fundamentals all the way up to epic project cakes and everything in between. We've filled it with our favourite bakes: some are unforgettable, unmistakable Crumbs & Doilies classics, and many of them are brand spanking new, just for you. Whatever you decide to bake, you can be sure that it is going to work, it's going to be fun and it's going to taste amazing!

Let's start at the beginning... I developed a sweet tooth at a very early age, but I was always happy for my treats to come in packets and wrappers until an impromptu stab at baking while travelling in Australia piqued my interest. When I came home, I began baking at every chance I got. I loved the process of baking: the precision, the variety, the opportunity to be creative with flavour and decoration. Most of all, I loved to share the experience of a great bake with others. I'd only ever worked in hospitality until then and giving people a great experience was my thing! Baking and sharing cakes felt like a truer, purer and more personal version of this. Seeing people's faces light up mid-way through a bite of something I'd made satisfied me on a whole new level, so it felt like the most natural move in the world to quit my job and start selling cakes.

Crumbs & Doilies began as a market stall on Brick Lane in April 2006. I'd spent months and countless hours testing, tweaking and perfecting my cupcakes and brownies and I was ready! I packed up my old banger of a car (a blue Ford Fiesta with a hole in the floor, which meant my feet got wet when it rained) and schlepped over to the market stall to sell my wares, having frantically but lovingly baked them the previous day. By closing time I'd sold out and, despite having sore feet, I was beaming!

Over time, my customers began to ask me to bake for their parties, weddings and events. I would scribble my number down on little paper doilies to give to people and it wasn't long before I was baking every day between market days to keep up with the orders. Sam, my partner at the time, had been helping out on the stall and in the kitchen, and in his spare time he built a website so that I could start selling cupcakes online. Soon the orders flooded in, so much so that Sam quit his job and came to work at Crumbs & Doilies full time.

Four years later, we'd outgrown our home operation and having cupcake paraphernalia bursting out of every drawer or cupboard in our tiny flat became intolerable, so we moved to a commercial space in Wandsworth and built the bakery - a 1,200-square-foot space that we rattled around in at first. It was a terrifyingly big move, but Sam and I were determined to grow our little cake stall into a proper business. We worked long hours, developed countless new recipes and grew

our tiny team to help with our burgeoning workload. Using the best ingredients and baking in small batches, we would never let anything leave the bakery unless it was perfect. Slowly but surely, our menu - and our reputation - began to grow.

Sam had begun a Crumbs & Doilies blog a few years earlier. Social media was still relatively new, but we soon gained an international following of fellow baking enthusiasts, and people who simply enjoyed seeing what we were working on. We were slap bang in the middle of a lovely global community, largely made up of people who loved what we did, despite often never having seen, let alone eaten, one of our cakes in real life. When I was approached by Jamie Oliver to start a YouTube channel under his Food Tube umbrella in 2013, having met him a couple of years earlier, I had no idea how much that community would grow. But uploading my weekly recipe tutorials really seemed to touch a lot of people and it wasn't long before the Cupcake Jemma channel had over a million subscribers. Growing and being part of this worldwide baking community quickly overshadowed any reservations we'd had about sharing our secrets with the world and we were thrilled to see people making our recipes, sharing their bakes with friends and tagging us in their photos.

Opening a shop had always been our dream. It wasn't just the appeal of a space that we could sell our cupcakes from, that wasn't a freezing cold or rainy market stall.

We desperately wanted somewhere to call home, a permanent space that was totally us, where people could come and try our bakes (in the warm), enjoy a coffee and hang out with us! After years of baking, saving and searching, we were ready, and took the lease on a tiny shop tucked away on a cobbled side-alley in the heart of Soho. We transformed this once-shabby, poky nail bar into a perfectly formed cake shop, with a mini bakery upstairs in which we could bake everything fresh each day for our customers. In December 2015, we threw open the door, and since then it's become a destination for people who make short and sometimes very long trips to meet the gang and try our cupcakes, cookies, brownies and bakes.

These days, Crumbs & Doilies has grown from just me and Sam to a family of wonderful, talented and devoted individuals, who work tirelessly across our HQ bakery, the Soho shop and, more recently, the Cupcake Jemma studio. Many have been with us for years, like Sally, Nikki, Dane, Rosie and Kevin, and the bakers, the front of house gang, office peeps and delivery drivers, both past and present, have all played a huge part in making Crumbs & Doilies the success it is today. The wheels keep turning thanks to the relentless efforts of Sam, helped enormously by our long-suffering but endlessly hard-working friend and colleague, Sally. You may also know these two to be a huge part of the Cupcake Jemma channel, with Sam being the one behind the camera and Sally often being in front of it with me! We have grown through sheer determination and hard work, despite me having no formal training in baking, neither Sam nor I having any experience of running a business, and with no bank loans or investment at all.

I hope our story encourages you, not only to bake, but also to push on and follow your passions, even if you think you don't have the credentials. At the very least, I hope you have fun baking from our book, are inspired to take what you learn and trust yourself to experiment with new ideas, and that it encourages you to connect with people through your baking. You are now part of our community and it's the friendliest, tastiest place on earth!

ESSENTIAL KIT

If you're a seasoned baker, there is a good chance you already have some, if not all, of the following. It may seem like a lot of stuff, but much of it is affordable and can have a huge impact on your baking. Here are our essentials that we use almost every day in the bakery and couldn't do without.

STAND MIXER

A stand mixer will save you a lot of time and effort. If you're someone who bakes often, it's a worthy investment. Look for a heavy, sturdy machine with at least the paddle and balloon whisk attachments.

ELECTRIC HAND MIXER

At the very least you need an inexpensive electric hand mixer, the kind that plugs in and has two pronged beaters. Even if you have a stand mixer, you will still find one useful for mixing up small quantities of things like buttercream and cream.

FOOD PROCESSOR

Pulverising, chopping, whizzing and wazzing... a food processor is an investment, for sure, but you can also get away with using some of the smaller machines, like Nutribullets and blenders.

MIXING BOWLS

Get lots of bowls: one or two quite big mixing bowls, a couple of medium-sized ones and loads of small ones for prepping ingredients.

DIGITAL SCALES

For me, these are non-negotiable! I don't do cup measures as there is so much room for error when you measure your ingredients by volume. I weigh pretty much everything, even liquids!

SPOON MEASURES

There's a time and a place for volumes. Get a proper set of measuring spoons, which include: 1 tablespoon, 1 teaspoon, ½ teaspoon and ¼ teaspoon measures. All spoon measurements in this book are 'level', unless otherwise instructed.

20CM/8IN SANDWICH TINS

We bake our four-layer cakes in four separate sandwich tins, for a shorter baking time, a more even bake and less crusty bits. Try to get four identical tins, either solid or loose-bottomed.

LOOSE-BOTTOMED SQUARE TIN

All the brownie recipes in this book are for a 20cm/8in square tin, which we find the perfect size for home baking. A loose-bottomed one makes removing your bakes easier and less stressful. Look for a high-sided tin with square corners, to ensure a neat finish.

12-HOLE CUPCAKE TIN

One or two cupcake tins should be plenty for the home-baker. Look for cupcake tins specifically, not 'muffin pans', which can be much deeper, or 'fairy cake' pans, which are usually a lot shallower.

PAPER CASES

Look for cases that fit your cupcake tin snugly. Foil cases tend to make your cupcakes crispy round the edges and 'novelty' ones can end up looking greasy. We prefer to use simple white paper cases.

OVEN GLOVES

A good set of oven gloves is so much safer than using a tea towel! Make sure you get ones that are thick but flexible, so you can curve your hands around the edges of tins and baking trays without any mishaps.

SAUCEPANS

A set of well-made, heavy-based pans will give the best heat distribution and last a lifetime. Avoid ones with a non-stick coating, if possible.

BAIN-MARIE

A glass or metal bowl set over a saucepan of simmering water will provide a gentle heat, perfect for melting chocolate or making curd. Make sure your water doesn't touch the bottom of the bowl.

BAKING TRAYS

Two good-quality, sturdy baking trays with a small rim around the edge will be useful. Always line your trays with greaseproof paper for easy removal and clean-up.

OVEN THERMOMETER

Every oven bakes differently and can vary by up to 20°C from the dial temperature. An oven thermometer will tell you if you need to adjust your settings as well as helping to identify any hot spots.

DIGITAL TIMER

A digital timer is accurate, easy to use and easy to read. Get one with a loud beep!

SUGAR THERMOMETER

A sugar thermometer is essential for tempering chocolate or making caramels. Make sure when you're using one that it's making contact with the hot liquid, rather than the bottom of the pan.

SIEVE

Sifting flour will make your bakes lighter and lump-free. One regular sieve is plenty, but an extra-fine sieve for straining and a tiny one for dusting will also be useful.

WHISK

Look for a whisk with strong metal loops with a good connection to the handle. Get a mini whisk too, for whisking smaller amounts of liquid.

ROLLING PIN

I'm a big fan of wooden rolling pins but they can also be made from marble (great for pastry as they stay cool) and plastic (these are usually non-stick). I'd recommend getting two: one regular rolling pin and one mini for fiddlier jobs.

RUBBER SPATULAS

A flexy rubber spatula is just the thing for scraping, stirring and scooping. Try to get yourself a mix of sizes, preferably heatproof.

WOODEN SPOON

Wooden spoons are sturdy, lightweight and perfect for all sorts of stirring. Make sure you get a couple, and at least one with a nice long handle for making caramel.

SHARP KNIVES

Make sure you have one 20–25cm/8–10in chef's knife, a medium 13–15cm/5–6in knife, a paring knife and a serrated bread knife.

MICROPLANE GRATER

A Microplane is so much sharper and faster to use than a regular grater. Get a fine one, which will be perfect for zesting fruit, shaving chocolate and grating nutmeg.

GREASEPROOF PAPER & SILPATS

The various types of baking paper do pretty much the same thing, but do take the time to cut it to the right size for your tin and use scissors! Silpats are great for cookies and brittles but not so great for meringues.

COOLING RACK

This will speed up the cooling of your cakes and bakes and prevent them getting soggy or stuck in their tins. It will also help ensure a crispy bottom on a cookie stays crisp.

AIRTIGHT CONTAINERS

Get a wide variety of different airtight containers, so you can store cakes, cookies and leftovers. The stacking kind are great as they take up less room in your cupboards.

CAKE LEVELLER

This wire suspended between a thin metal rod is unmatched for the job of levelling and splitting sponges. It can be adjusted to create different thicknesses and is essential if you want to end up with a perfectly straight cake.

CAKE RINGS/COOKIE CUTTERS

We recommend getting a good set of nesting cookie cutters ranging from a couple of inches in diameter up to 18cm/7in, for jobs such as cake trimming and cookie chomping!

TURNTABLE

For a lovely smooth, straight-sided finish on the top and sides of your cakes, a turntable will make it a whole lot easier to achieve.

APPLE CORER

The perfect tool for making holes in your cupcakes for filling.

PIPING BAGS

Large 35-40cm/14-16in piping bags are great for distributing cake batter and buttercream. Smaller 20-25cm/8-10in ones are perfect for dripping ganache and filling cupcakes with goo. Reusable bags are sturdy enough to be used again and again. Get a few of each size.

PIPING NOZZLES

There are hundreds of kinds of nozzles. The ones we use the most are a large round one (16mm diameter) and a 6-point open star of a similar size for decorating cupcakes and applying small blobs, stars and ruffles to the tops of cakes. See the QR code on page 72 to learn more about them.

PALETTE KNIVES

A small offset (cranked) palette knife stops your knuckles dragging through icing as you decorate. A large, straight palette knife is brilliant for applying larger amounts of icing onto cakes for quick, even crumb-coats and topcoats. I recommend you get one of each.

CAKE SCRAPER

We prefer plastic scrapers with a straight edge to smooth out the icing on the sides and tops of layer cakes. Check out the QR code on page 210 to see this in action.

KITCHEN BLOWTORCH

For a professional finish to Italian meringue. They are also useful for heating your knife before you cut into bakes, for super-clean slices. Check that your target is on a heatproof surface and there are no tea towels or kitchen roll nearby.

ESSENTIAL INGREDIENTS

With supermarkets selling almost every variation of every kind of food out there, it can be tricky to know where to start when you shop for baking ingredients. However, there are some things that you should just always have in your cupboard if you like to get your bake on. Here are the ones we couldn't do without.

―――

UNSALTED BUTTER

I love butter. There's very little I won't put it on or in. The only butter we would ever bake with is unsalted butter, with a fat content of 82–84%. The lack of salt means you get to control the flavour and add salt as you see fit and the high fat content ensures the butter acts in the best interest of your bakes. Butter is NOT the same as margarine or spreadable butter and I might not forgive you if you are using these instead. Buy the best butter you can afford. Better Butter Begets Better Baking!

SUGAR

There are so many different types of sugar, which are all useful for different things. Here are the ones we use most in the bakery and what they do:

Caster Sugar: A white sugar with a fine grain. Not to be confused with granulated sugar, which has a bigger grain and therefore doesn't dissolve easily. It adds sweetness but not flavour and dissolves quickly, so it's perfect for sponges, meringues and caramel.

Icing Sugar: A super-fine, white powdered sugar. Sometimes called confectioners' sugar, it dissolves almost instantaneously when mixed with liquid, making it great for glazes, and is an essential ingredient in light, fluffy buttercream. Always sift icing sugar before working with it as there are often lumps in the packets. If you find that your buttercream is a little grainy no matter how long you beat it for, try a different brand with a different anti-caking agent.

Soft Brown Sugar: Slightly moist sugar with a medium grain. Soft light and dark brown sugars are rich, slightly sticky sugars with a pleasing caramel flavour, which add a gooey, chewy texture to cookies. It's a good idea to sieve brown sugar first, as sometimes it can be a little clumpy straight out of the packet.

Muscovado Sugar: An unrefined sugar with a medium grain and a sticky texture. Both light and dark muscovado sugars still contain most of or all their molasses, giving them the most intensely rich, treacly caramel flavour that is perfect in recipes like sticky toffee sauce.

Demerara Sugar: A very coarse grain, granulated brown sugar. Demerara is best used to add texture and crunch. It has a pleasing, light molasses flavour and is great sprinkled on cookies and muffins before baking and even on top of cupcakes as a decoration.

FLOUR

There are lots of different kinds of flours available. The ones we use in the bakery are plain and self-raising wheat flour. Plain flour, also known as all-purpose flour, is a finely milled wheat flour which produces light bakes. Self-raising flour is essentially plain flour with a raising agent added to help bakes to rise. If you find self-raising flour difficult to get where you are, you can make a version of it yourself by adding 2 tsp baking powder for every 150g of plain flour. This can add a slightly bitter, salty flavour though, so if a recipe calls for self-raising flour, do try to use it.

RAISING AGENTS

There are two main ingredients that we use to create a bit of lift in our bakes when we aren't relying solely on beating air into the batter. The first is bicarbonate of soda, which is best used when there is some acidity in the bake, as it reacts and fizzes when mixed with any kind of acid. Things like milk, buttermilk, lemon, vinegar, and even chocolate and cocoa powder, will have enough acidity to allow the bicarb to do its thing. The second is baking powder, which is simply bicarb with a little bit of acid built in. This is good for those bakes that don't have any or much acidity in the rest of the ingredients. You often need to use quite a bit of baking powder compared to bicarb to get a good lift, so we occasionally combine the two.

EGGS

We use large, free-range, organic eggs for our recipes and I hope you will too. You will notice the difference in the quality of flavour, colour and texture when you bake with eggs from happier hens, instead of their unfortunate, battery-housed relatives.

All mentions of egg in this book are large eggs. If you can only get your hands on medium or small eggs, don't worry. A large egg (out of its shell) weighs around 60g, so tot up the amount of eggs you need for a recipe (e.g. 3 eggs = 180g) and weigh your small or medium eggs into a bowl to get the correct total egg weight (whisking them first will make this a lot easier).

SEA SALT

We make sweet food, but we often add salt to our bakes. This might seem counterintuitive, but adding salt, particularly sea salt, will enhance the flavours of your ingredients and make them sing. Beware of using table salt, as its higher sodium level will simply add saltiness, whereas the lower sodium and retained minerals in sea salt will carry more flavour to your taste buds.

MILK & CREAM

When baking with dairy, always try to use products with the highest fat content, rather than low-fat versions. Butter, milk, cream and cream cheese are at their very best in all their full-fat glory and have enough fat in them to do what you need them to do in a bake, such as whipping up to be light and fluffy. They also have the added benefit of tasting better!

GLUTEN-FREE FLOUR

Many of the recipes in this book can be made using a gluten-free flour blend, such as the ones made by Doves Farm. It works well when replacing the flour in cupcakes and cakes, but you may need to add a little xanthan gum to help bind the batter and give it a little more 'bounce'. If substituting flour for gluten-free flour, use ¼ tsp xanthan gum for the cupcake recipes in this book and 1 tsp for the cake recipes.

COFFEE

It might sound crazy but putting coffee into chocolate cake makes it taste even chocolatier. I urge you to put aside any scepticism and just use the coffee! It's always best to use brewed, cooled coffee in your sponge, but you can also use instant, if that's all you have. But when a recipe calls for espresso, use espresso! In the likely event that you don't own an espresso machine, nip to your local coffee shop and pick up some shots to take away.

COCOA POWDER

We use Dutch-processed cocoa powder in the bakery. This is cocoa that has been alkalised and therefore has a less acidic, bitter flavour than its 'natural' counterpart. It's much darker in colour with a more mellow and well-rounded flavour. If you like a super-dark chocolate bake though, get your mitts on some black cocoa powder. It's gone through even more Dutch processing and is therefore way darker and more intense than any other cocoa out there. We use it in our Double Chocolate NY Cookies for a bit more chocolatey drama.

VANILLA

If you want your bakes to taste next-level delicious, use a good-quality vanilla extract. We use a glucose-based extract that is packed full of vanilla seeds, rather than a thin alcohol-based one, as the flavour is far superior. Avoid vanilla essence at all costs!

FOOD COLOURING

These days, there's lots of choice and variety in food colourings as well as hundreds of colours to choose from. However, avoid the liquid stuff. It's not concentrated enough to achieve vibrant colours in your bakes and icings – you need so much of it that it would change the consistency and flavour of your bakes. There are only two you should be using:

Gel/paste colour: (Sugarflair and AmeriColor do a great range of colours) These can be used for anything from colouring sponges and buttercreams to adding to meringues and marshmallows.

Oil-based colour: (AmeriColor and Colour Mill are our faves) Can be used to colour white chocolate as well as sponges and buttercreams, but don't work at all for meringues.

CHOCOLATE

Good-quality chocolate can come at a price, but you won't regret spending the extra pennies when you eat your bakes. A great chocolate can transform a decent brownie into an exceptional one! We use four different kinds of base chocolate in the bakery, all with a different percentage of cocoa solids.

Dark (70% cocoa solids): This has an intense, slightly bitter, unmistakably chocolatey flavour. It's brilliant for adding to brownies, cake batter and buttercream when you want a strong chocolate hit without any added sweetness.

Dark (50–65% cocoa solids): Still has the intensity of dark chocolate, but is smoother and less bitter, making it our go-to for ganache and chocolate chips in cookies.

Milk (30–34% cocoa solids): Great for dipping cookies in, using as chocolate chips, or in a ganache that will give you a sweet, creamy flavour and probably remind you of your childhood.

White chocolate (25-30% cocoa butter):
Sweet, often vanilla-enhanced and creamy, this makes a great addition as chocolate chips, but also is the base for one of our favourite inclusions: Caramelised White Chocolate (see page 54).

TEMPERING CHOCOLATE

Taking the time to temper your chocolate, rather than shoving it in the microwave just to get hot and runny, will result in a chocolate that sets at room temperature. Untempered chocolate will go cloudy or bloom over time and, when you need to coat a cookie, cupcake or cake ball, it will stay soft and sticky at room temperature, resulting in very messy fingers. Tempered chocolate will also have a pleasing crack when you break it or bite into it. There are a few ways to temper chocolate and it can be quite technical, but I've given you two ways of doing it here. The proper way using a bain-marie, ice bath and thermometer, and the cheat's way, where you just use your wits (this technically isn't tempering but with a bit of practice can produce brilliant results!).

The proper way

Prepare a bain-marie (see page 13) and also an ice bath by filling a larger bowl with ice. Measure your chocolate chips. Remove a third from the bowl, chop these up finely and set aside. Heat the remaining chocolate in the bain-marie, stirring occasionally. Use a thermometer to help you get it to the first temperature noted in the range above right. Remove from the heat and stir in the reserved chocolate chips until they have melted completely. Place this bowl into the ice bath and stir constantly, checking with the thermometer, until you reach the second temperature in the range. Once you hit that, return the bowl to the pan of simmering

water and heat gently, stirring constantly until you reach the third and final temperature.

Dark chocolate: 1st – 50–55°C; 2nd – 28°C; 3rd – 31°C

Milk chocolate: 1st – 45–50°C; 2nd – 27°C; 3rd – 29°C

White chocolate: 1st – 45–50°C; 2nd – 26°C; 3rd – 28°C

The cheat's way

Measure your chocolate chips. Remove a third of them and chop these a bit finer, then set aside. In a bain-marie over a low heat, or in the microwave in 10-second bursts, stirring in between, melt the larger amount of chocolate until it is almost melted but has a few small nuggets still knocking about. Remove from the heat or microwave and add the chopped chocolate chips, then stir, stir, stir, stir, STIR until all of the chips have melted completely.

KITCHEN RULES

Your kitchen – your rules ... buuuut, if you want to get set up for success, I highly recommend you follow a few of ours. We've been at this for a long time. Some of our bakers are classically trained, some are self-taught like me, but we can all agree that the following rules are essential to a smooth-running and happy kitchen.

――――

READ THE RECIPE
Read the whole recipe before you begin, to avoid unwanted surprises. You don't want to realise you haven't got everything you need, or enough time to complete the process, when you're midway through.

GET PREPPED
There's a fancy term for this – 'mise en place'. Sorting, weighing and measuring your ingredients before you begin baking will save you time and prevent mistakes. Finding out you haven't got enough flour halfway through baking a cake, or filling your house with smoke because your caramel is burning as you find and measure out your cream, is less than ideal. Get prepped!

WORK CLEAN
Keeping your workstation clean and tidy can transform the experience of baking from kind of stressful and haphazard to enjoyable and mindful. Wash up as you go, keep a clean cloth nearby so that you can wipe your work surface whenever required, and wash your hands regularly rather than simply wiping them on your apron (or your clothes!). A tidy kitchen = a tidy mind.

TASTE AS YOU GO
Taste your buttercreams, bakes, caramels (once they're cool) or goos and use your judgement. If you think your bakes need more salt, add more salt. If your buttercream would taste better to you with more raspberry goo in it, put more in. Everyone's taste is different, so adjust things if you want to.

DON'T BE AFRAID TO EXPERIMENT
We've spent a lot of time perfecting these recipes. We know that they work and taste fantastic, but if you want to mix things up or experiment with different flavour combos and additions, you don't need our permission to do so. The Basics & BFFs chapter is a great source of recipes that you can mix and match, so have a go!

I SAID EXPERIMENT, NOT DESTROY!
While I encourage you to be creative, there is also a limit to how much changing a recipe can take! There's a good reason for the amount of sugar and butter in a recipe, for example. Baking is science and some things just won't work as well if you halve the amount of sugar because the recipe seems too sweet to you. Get to know when to swap ingredients and when to leave things alone.

MAKE NOTES
Whenever you are tweaking, testing, experimenting and altering recipes, it's a good idea to have a notepad and pen

handy so that you can note down what you did and whether it worked or not, to enable you to recreate your successful bake again and again.

SOFTEN YOUR BUTTER

Butter that is either too soft or not soft enough will often have a dramatic and undesirable impact on your cakes and buttercreams. 'Softened' doesn't mean room temperature (your room might be 40°C, or it might be 12°C, neither of which is ideal!). Test your butter for perfect softness by pressing a finger into it. It should give way easily and your finger should come away with only the thinnest film of butter on it, rather than being covered in the stuff! A few hours at an ambient temperature should get it there, but if you're in a rush, you can ping your butter in the microwave in 3–5-second bursts, stirring it in between to achieve the perfect softness.

GET TO KNOW YOUR OVEN

Most ovens have hot and cool spots and lie about their temperature. I highly recommend buying an oven thermometer, testing your oven temperatures and adjusting your settings accordingly. All of the recipes in this book are for the 'real' temperature inside your oven and not necessarily the one on the dial. To test for hot spots, it's worth knocking up a batch of cupcakes. You will see from the colour on the tops where your oven is getting too hot or not hot enough. If you have a particularly uneven oven, I recommend turning your bakes by 180°, two-thirds of the way through the baking time, to ensure you get a more even bake.

WHEN TO REMOVE YOUR SPONGES

You'll notice that we are quite specific with our instructions to remove the sponges from the tins in the Cakes section. Take heed!

If you try to remove your sponge too soon, while it is still hot, it will be too fragile and is likely to break. If you leave it until it's completely cool, there is a good chance that the cake will re-set, causing it to get stuck and break. The best time to remove the sponge is when it's had a chance to settle and cool a little, but is still warm. This should result in sponges that pop out easily when you turn the tin upside down.

SCALING RECIPES UP AND DOWN

You may want to scale recipes up or down to fit the number of people you need to serve. If a recipe calls for a 'half batch', divide all the ingredients by two. If a recipe calls for a 'double batch', multiply everything by two! The only sticking point might be with eggs, but you can split an egg by weighing it in a bowl, dividing that weight by two, and whisking up the egg to combine the white and yolk, which will make it much easier to pour out half.

KEEP YOUR LEFTOVERS

Whether it's scraps from trimmed cakes, the removed insides of cupcakes, egg whites or yolks that have been separated and not used, or little bits of leftover buttercream or goo, always keep your leftovers. You never know when they might come in handy for nibbling or knocking up a quick bake on a whim! Make sure you use airtight containers, and label and date them for easy identification.

BASICS
& BFFS

BASICS & BFFS

Everyone needs to have their BFFs around them and these are some of ours. In this chapter I'll take you through some of the essential recipes that we use in the Crumbs & Doilies bakery, day in, day out, as the building blocks for so many of our bakes. Sure, you can grab raspberry jam or meringues from the supermarket, but if you want to knock people's socks off with flavourful, perfectly textured, interesting and enticing bakes, then baking from scratch is the way to go. With classic vanilla and chocolate sponges, different types of buttercreams and icings, and some of our favourite additions, like pie crumb and fruit goo, you'll soon be baking like a pro!

This chapter is aimed at giving you confidence and kitting you out with a toolbox of recipes that you'll keep coming back to time and time again. Some of the recipes in this book might seem daunting at first, but when you break them down into their individual elements, you'll realise they aren't all that difficult. With these Basics & BFFs you will not only be able to make the recipes in here, but I hope you will also experiment with them to create new and exciting combinations that are unique to you. With essential tips and tricks straight from the Crumbs & Doilies bakery team, you'll have everything you need to start your baking journey or build on your existing skills.

Preparing a cake tin

Filling and using piping bags

Pooping meringues

VANILLA SPONGE 26

VANILLA CUPCAKES 28

CHOCOLATE SPONGE 30

CHOCOLATE CUPCAKES 32

C&D CHOCOLATE BROWNIE 34

BASIC BUTTERCREAM 36

CREAM CHEESE ICING 38

SWISS MERINGUE BUTTERCREAM 40

SALTED CARAMEL 42

SALTED CARAMEL BUTTERCREAM 44

FRENCH MERINGUES (POOPS) 45

ITALIAN MERINGUE 48

CRÈME PÂTISSIÈRE & MOUSSELINE 50

CHOCOLATE GANACHE 52

CARAMELISED WHITE CHOCOLATE 54

BURNT BUTTER 56

LEMON CURD 58

GOO 60

NUT BUTTER 62

PIE CRUMB 64

COOKIE DOUGH 66

MALTY CORNFLAKES 68

Makes a 20cm/8in,
4-layer cake to
serve 12-16

500g caster sugar
135g vegetable oil
330g unsalted butter,
softened

8 eggs
500g self-raising flour
6 tbsp milk
1 tsp vanilla extract

VANILLA SPONGE

If you're just starting out on your baking journey, the chances are that a basic vanilla sponge is one of the first things you try. So let's make it a good one! Soft, fluffy and moist, you'll keep coming back to simple bakes like this again and again.

Preheat your oven to 190°C (170°C fan) and grease four 20cm/8in round cake tins.

Put the sugar, oil and butter into a stand mixer fitted with the paddle attachment, or a large mixing bowl, and beat on medium–high speed for a couple of minutes. This is where we are creating most of the air for this cake, so beating it for long enough at this stage is crucial. Your mixture should be light in colour and very fluffy, almost doubled in size.

Add the eggs two at a time, beating well after each addition. The mixture might look a bit curdled, but this has very little effect on the end result, so don't worry about it!

Sift the flour directly on top of the mixture and fold in, either on the lowest speed on the mixer or by hand using a large metal spoon, being careful not to be too rough and knock out the air.

When all of the flour has mostly been incorporated into the batter, add the milk and vanilla and fold or mix it through carefully until everything is well combined.

Distribute the batter evenly among the tins. (If you want to be 'extra', do this precisely using digital scales – yet another good reason to get some!) Level out the tops with a palette knife and bake for 22-24 minutes until a skewer comes out completely clean from the centre of each sponge (make sure you check them all as your oven might be a bit uneven).

Once baked, remove from the oven and leave to cool for 15–20 minutes before removing the sponges from their tins. Set a timer for this. If you do it when they are too hot, they're in danger of breaking; too cold and they might stick in the tins.

Your sponges are ready! Trim, fill, crumb-coat, and decorate in whatever way you fancy. For tips on how to do this, head to page 210.

Makes 12

125g unsalted
    butter, softened
125g caster sugar
125g self-raising flour
2 eggs

¼ tsp bicarbonate
    of soda
1½ tbsp milk
¼ tsp vanilla extract

VANILLA CUPCAKES

When I started Crumbs & Doilies, I spent forever perfecting my Vanilla Cupcake recipe to make sure it was easy to do, consistent and – of course – delicious. We have tweaked it even more in the bakery over the years, so this is a recipe you can rely on to work every time.

———

Preheat your oven to 190°C (170°C fan) and line a 12-hole cupcake tin with paper cases.

In the bowl of a stand mixer fitted with the paddle attachment, or a medium mixing bowl if you're using an electric hand mixer (or a wooden spoon if you fancy a workout), beat the butter, sugar, flour, eggs and bicarb, starting off slowly to combine the ingredients, then cranking up to a medium speed and beating for around 30 seconds (more like 5 minutes, if you're using a spoon) until the ingredients are well combined and smooth.

Stop the mixer and add the milk and vanilla, then beat again for a few seconds. Stop and scrape the sides and bottom of the bowl to bring any bits that got missed back into the mixture. Beat again for 30 seconds to incorporate the stragglers and you should have a lovely smooth batter.

Using a pair or spoons or a piping bag, fill the paper cases about three-quarters full to use up all of the batter. If you want to see this in action, head to the QR code on page 24.

Bake for 18–20 minutes, or until the tops bounce back when pressed lightly with a finger.

Remove from the oven and leave the cakes to cool completely before decorating with your choice of buttercream.

Makes a 20cm/
8in, 4-layer cake
to serve 12-16

650g plain flour
690g caster sugar
120g cocoa powder
2 tsp bicarbonate
 of soda

1 tsp sea salt
6 eggs
450g coffee, cooled
450g buttermilk
390g vegetable oil

CHOCOLATE SPONGE

We use this rich, moist cake as the basis for so many of our cakes. It's so easy to make! You don't need any fancy equipment, just a couple of big bowls and a whisk, and it stays moist for ages, which means it's a great cake to make ahead of time.

———

Preheat your oven to 190°C (170°C fan). Grease and/or line four 20cm/8in round cake tins.

Sift the flour, sugar, cocoa, bicarb and salt into a large bowl and set aside.

In your largest bowl (this makes a lot of batter!), whisk together the eggs, coffee, buttermilk and oil. It will look a bit curdled, but that's fine.

Tip all of the dry ingredients into the wet mixture and whisk together until you have a smooth, lump-free, runny batter. Distribute the batter evenly among the cake tins and put two tins on both of two evenly spaced shelves in the oven. Bake for 24–30 minutes until a skewer comes out clean from the centre of all of the sponges (check them all in case your oven bakes unevenly).

Remove from the oven and leave to cool for 15–20 minutes before removing the sponges from the tins.

Decorate your cake however you like – the possibilities are endless! For tips on trimming, levelling and decorating your cakes perfectly, head to the QR codes on page 210.

140g plain flour
185g caster sugar
35g cocoa powder
¼ tsp sea salt

½ tsp bicarbonate
  of soda
35g dark chocolate
  chips (54% cocoa
  solids), finely chopped

2 eggs
125g coffee, cold
125g buttermilk
105g vegetable oil

CHOCOLATE CUPCAKES

Our delivery driver, Kevin, hasn't got much of a sweet tooth. But if there's one thing he can't resist, it's a naked chocolate cupcake. No icing, no extras. Just as it is. These babies are moist, just rich enough without being overly sweet and an absolute doddle to make. And if you're not Kevin, why not try topping them with our favourite Chocolate Cream Cheese Icing (page 38).

Preheat your oven to 170°C (150°C fan) and line a 12-hole cupcake tin with paper cases.

In a medium bowl, sift together the flour, sugar, cocoa, salt and bicarb, then add the chocolate chips and whisk to combine.

In a separate, larger bowl, combine the eggs, coffee, buttermilk and vegetable oil and whisk together. It will look a little weird and curdled but that's okay – the dry ingredients will sort that out.

Add the dry mixture to the bowl of wet ingredients and thoroughly whisk together until you have a lovely thick, runny batter that would be smooth if it weren't for the chocolate chips!

Using a jug to help you pour, divide the batter among the paper cases and bake for 20–22 minutes until the tops spring back when touched lightly with your finger.

Remove from the oven and leave to cool completely before decorating with your choice of icing.

Basics & BFFs

Makes a 20cm/8in brownie to serve 9–16, depending on the size of your squares

165g unsalted butter
165g dark chocolate
(70% cocoa solids)
3 eggs

330g caster sugar
1 tsp vanilla extract
135g plain flour
45g cocoa powder

½ tsp sea salt
½ tsp baking powder

C&D CHOCOLATE BROWNIE

Everybody needs a go-to brownie recipe. This is ours, and I hope it will soon be yours! The cocoa powder makes this brownie extra rich, fudgy and ever-so-slightly chewy. And, while this is the perfect base for some of the brownie recipes later in the book, it's also amazing just as it is.

———

Preheat your oven to 190°C (170°C fan) and grease and line a high-sided 20cm/8in square tin.

Melt the butter and chocolate together, either in a microwave in 30-second bursts, or gently over a bain-marie, and stir to combine. Leave to cool for 5–10 minutes.

In a separate bowl, whisk together the eggs and sugar for a few minutes until they have doubled in volume and turned quite pale. Add the melted chocolate mixture, stirring as you go, then add the vanilla and fold in slowly.

Set a sieve over the bowl and sift in all of the dry ingredients, then fold in carefully to make a thick, smooth batter.

Pour the batter into the prepared tin, levelling the mixture with a spoon or a palette knife if necessary.

Bake for 28–30 minutes until your brownies are just set and a skewer comes out a bit gooey when poked. This is how we bake our brownies at Crumbs & Doilies, and that's how we think you should bake them too! However, we appreciate that some of you may like a more 'cakey' brownie. If that's you, no judgement! Just keep it in for a minute or two longer.

Leave to cool (or not quite if you like to eat your brownie a bit warm), then remove from the tin and slice into squares.

———

TEAM TIP
Put your brownie in the fridge overnight (or for at least a few hours) for the ultimate fudgy, dense and fully set brownie. Then, cut it into squares and dig in.

34

Makes enough to ice
12 regular cupcakes;
double the quantity to
fill, crumb-coat and ice a
4-layer, 20cm/8in cake

285g unsalted
  butter, softened
¼ tsp sea salt
450g icing
  sugar, sifted

¼ tsp vanilla extract
1½ tbsp whole milk

BASIC BUTTERCREAM

One of the most common questions we're asked is: how do we get our classic vanilla buttercream so white? The secret: it's all in the beating! A batch of buttercream should take 10-15 minutes if you're using a stand mixer and even longer if you're making it by hand. The pay-off is light, white, fluffy, smooth buttercream.

———

In the bowl of a stand mixer fitted with the paddle attachment or a medium mixing bowl, beat the butter and salt together on a high speed for at least 5 minutes until the butter has turned a very pale yellow and the texture is smooth and whippy.

Add half of the icing sugar and bring together on a slow speed to avoid plumes of sugar jumping out of the bowl, then beat vigorously for a few minutes before repeating with the remaining icing sugar. Beat until you have a pale, almost white, fluffy mixture.

Beat in the vanilla, then the milk, a little at a time. Depending on the softness of your butter and the temperature of your kitchen, you might not need to add all of the milk, or you may even need a bit more. You're looking for a smooth, whippy buttercream that has a spreadable consistency and holds its shape.

VARIATIONS
Here are some alternatives to vanilla. Just replace the milk and vanilla with the following additional ingredients to mix things up a bit!

Cherry – 1½ tbsp kirsch or cherry syrup
Espresso – 1½ tbsp strong espresso, cooled
Hazelnut – 1½ tbsp hazelnut butter
Lemon – 1½ tbsp freshly squeezed lemon juice
Raspberry/Blueberry/Strawberry – 1½ tbsp Goo (page 60)
Yuzu – 1½ tbsp yuzu juice
Cinnamon – keep milk and add ½ tsp ground cinnamon
Oreo – keep milk and add 4 tbsp finely crushed Oreo crumbs
Peanut Butter or Biscoff – beat 90g smooth peanut butter or Biscoff spread with the butter at the beginning

———

TEAM TIP
Store it in an airtight container at a cool room temperature for up to 4 days. Give it a really good whip before using and add a little milk if it's too stiff. If your buttercream is REALLY firm, then you can blast it in the microwave for 5-second bursts, but be warned, it will melt very easily, so go cautiously.

Makes enough to ice 12 regular cupcakes; double the quantity to fill, crumb-coat and ice a 4-layer, 20cm/8in cake

CREAM CHEESE ICING
125g unsalted butter, softened
¼ tsp sea salt
200g full-fat cream cheese
700g icing sugar, sifted

CHOCOLATE CREAM CHEESE ICING
55g unsalted butter, softened
¼ tsp sea salt
230g full-fat cream cheese

375g icing sugar, sifted
170g dark chocolate (70% cocoa solids), melted and cooled

CREAM CHEESE ICING

Cream cheese gives these icings a tang that makes them the perfect topping for any cakes that are fudgy or sweet, such as Chocolate or Red Velvet. The regular cream cheese icing is light and creamy, while the chocolate version is super rich without being heavy, and so delicious that we tend to use it in place of regular chocolate buttercream in the bakery these days. Ensure the cream cheese is at room temperature before using.

———

In the bowl of a stand mixer fitted with the paddle attachment, or a medium mixing bowl, beat the butter and salt together on a high speed until it goes pale and whippy.

Add the room-temperature cream cheese and beat together until lovely and smooth. It's quite important to use cream cheese that's at room temperature, or it will chill the butter as it mixes with it and you will end up with lumps of cold butter in your icing!

Add the sifted icing sugar in two stages, beating thoroughly after each addition, until you have a white, whippy, delicious icing.

FOR CHOCOLATE CREAM CHEESE ICING
Follow the method for regular cream cheese icing, then add the melted chocolate at the end and beat it in until it's really well combined. It is important that your melted chocolate isn't warm or (heaven forbid!) hot. If it is, it will melt the icing and you'll end up with a sloppy, liquid mess.

VARIATION
For an even creamier version, you can make this into mascarpone icing by replacing the regular cream cheese with mascarpone in the same quantity. This is delicious on cakes such as the Tiramisu Cake on page 221.

———

TEAM TIP
Like buttercream, you can make cream cheese icings in advance. Store in an airtight container at a cool room temperature for up to 4 days.

Makes enough to ice
12 regular cupcakes;
double the quantity to
fill, crumb-coat and ice a
4-layer, 20cm/8in cake

150g egg whites
300g caster sugar
360g unsalted butter,
  softened

¼ tsp sea salt
½ tsp vanilla extract

SWISS MERINGUE BUTTERCREAM

Swiss meringue buttercream makes a great alternative to regular buttercream. Not only is it smooth, silky and an absolute joy to work with, it's also slightly less sweet, which makes it a great icing for flavours that are already on the sweeter side.

In a bain-marie set over a medium heat, combine the egg whites and sugar, and stir slowly and continuously for 5–10 minutes or until all of the sugar has dissolved (check by rubbing some of the mixture between your thumb and forefinger). Don't rush this. If there are still grains at this point, you will have grainy, rather than silky buttercream. The mixture should reach between 60°C and 80°C for safe, stable meringue, which you can check with a sugar thermometer.

Transfer the mixture to the bowl of a stand mixer fitted with the balloon whisk attachment, or keep it in the bowl as you whisk with an electric hand mixer. Whisk on a high speed for 10–15 minutes, or until the mixture has come back down to room temperature and you have a lovely, glossy, bright white meringue with stiff peaks.

Whisk in the soft butter, a little nugget at a time, until all of the butter is in and you have a silky, luxuriously smooth buttercream. Add the salt and vanilla, and any other flavours you are using (see opposite for variations) and whisk to combine.

While it's best when just made, Swiss meringue buttercream will keep at room temperature for 2–4 days or in the fridge for up to a week. It will need to be brought to room temperature and whipped up a bit before using.

VARIATIONS
We use this recipe as the base for a variety of flavours in the bakery and throughout this book. Here are some of the ways you can switch it up. Just replace the vanilla with the following extras at the end of the process and stir thoroughly to combine.

Honey – 4 tbsp strongly flavoured honey
Strawberry/Raspberry/Blueberry – 4 tbsp Goo (page 60)
Matcha – 3 tsp matcha green tea powder (or to taste)
Milk/Dark/White Chocolate – 300g melted and slightly cooled chocolate
Pistachio – 2½ tbsp smooth pistachio paste
Biscoff – 300g Lotus Biscoff spread

TEAM TIP
Sometimes things can get a little bit sloppy when making Swiss meringue buttercream. Don't freak out. You can bring things back by using one or both of these suggestions: put the bowl into the fridge for a few minutes to chill down before whisking up again. Or, just keep whisking really fast – eventually it should come back around.

Basics & BFFs

Makes 310g, enough to use as both a filling and in the buttercream for 12 cupcakes

175g double cream
½ tsp vanilla extract
½ tsp sea salt (omit for regular caramel)

175g caster sugar
75ml water

SALTED CARAMEL

We always make this caramel in huge batches at the bakery because we use it in so many of our cakes and bakes. We fill cakes with it, drizzle with it, add it to icings and toppings... it's so useful to have around! But don't forget, making caramel of any kind means working with scalding hot, bubbling, sticky sugar, so make sure you have a big enough pan, a long-enough spoon and all of your ingredients ready so you don't have a mad dash to finish things off.

Measure the cream into a jug, then stir in the vanilla and salt, and set aside near your cooker.

Put the sugar and water into a medium saucepan and give it a stir to make sure the sugar is all soaked. Set over a low-medium heat and heat without stirring. It will begin to bubble, the sugar will dissolve, then after a few minutes it will start to caramelise.

When the mixture has turned a lovely rich amber colour, remove the pan from the heat and, very carefully, pour in the cream a little at a time, stirring quickly to combine until all of the cream is mixed through.

Leave to cool completely, before popping into the fridge in an airtight container.

TEAM TIPS
Stirring this kind of caramel as it cooks can cause the sugar to crystallise. If this happens, it is salvageable! Just turn the heat up a notch or two and move the pan around every now and then. Eventually, the crystals will break down again and caramelise.

Similarly, if your caramel turns into one giant sticky ball when you add the cream, don't freak out! Put the pan back over a low-medium heat and gently stir until the ball dissolves. You can also sieve the caramel (carefully!) to remove any hard nuggets or lumps.

The feeling of euphoria from successfully making caramel can quickly dissolve when you notice the pile of sticky caramel-covered equipment that it leaves behind. But don't fear! Put your messy utensils into the saucepan, fill it halfway with water, and return it to the hob over a low heat to melt off the caramel.

Basics & BFFs

Makes enough to ice 12 regular cupcakes; double the quantity to fill, crumb-coat and ice a 4-layer, 20cm/8in cake

200g unsalted butter, softened
320g icing sugar, sifted

½ x batch of Salted Caramel (see page 42)

SALTED CARAMEL BUTTERCREAM

One of our favourite things to do with the Salted Caramel on the previous page is to turn it into buttercream to use on our cakes and cupcakes. You'll find loads of ways to use it throughout this book, from Salted Caramel Pretzel Cupcakes (page 101) and Marathon Cake (page 251) to the epic S'mores Cake (page 230) and, of course, the Salted Caramel Cake (page 245), which is a celebration of all things salty and sweet!

In the bowl of a stand mixer fitter with the paddle attachment, or in a large mixing bowl, beat the butter on a high speed for around 5 minutes until it's pale and whippy.

Add the icing sugar in two batches and beat for 3–5 minutes after each addition.

Add the salted caramel and beat for a further 3 minutes until you have a light, fluffy, spreadable buttercream that holds its shape.

TEAM TIP
Sometimes you want your Caramel and Caramel Buttercream to be straight up caramel, no salt. That's okay. Just omit the salt when making it. You can always add it in at the end if you change your mind!

Basics & BFFs

Makes about 30–40 'poops' or 4–6 apple-sized messy meringues

70g egg whites (if you get any yolk in it, chuck it and start again, as this will kill your meringue!)

⅛ tsp cream of tartar
140g caster sugar
a pinch of sea salt
⅛ tsp vanilla extract (optional)

FRENCH MERINGUES (POOPS)

I'm afraid you're going to be reading a lot about poops in this recipe. We have always called meringue kisses 'poops' at C&D and it's one of those labels that has stuck, so apologies in advance if you aren't into the whole 'poop' thing!

This is a really straightforward recipe that results in crispy, slightly chewy meringues that you can use in loads of ways. Whipping the egg whites can take up to 15 minutes or more, so having a stand mixer will make your life a whole lot easier.

You always want twice the weight of sugar to egg whites, so the recipe below is just a guide, based on 2 large egg whites.

———

Preheat your oven to 120°C (100°C fan) and line one or two baking sheets with greaseproof paper. Firstly, make sure all of your equipment is clean and free from grease by rubbing it all with a little vinegar or lemon juice. Grease is the killer of fluffy, voluminous meringues.

Place the egg whites in the bowl of a stand mixer fitted with the balloon whisk attachment or a mixing bowl. Get it mixing on a low-medium speed. Once big bubbles start to form, you can add the cream of tartar and turn the mixer up to a medium-high speed.

Within a couple of minutes, the bubbles should be a lot smaller and tighter and if you were to pull the whisk out, the peaks would be soft and a bit floppy. Keep the mixer going on the same speed and begin to add the sugar a tablespoon at a time.

When all of the sugar has been added, keep whisking until you can no longer feel grains of sugar when you rub some of the mixture between your thumb and forefinger. This can take 10–15 minutes, sometimes more if you're making a big batch. Towards the end, add the salt and vanilla and whisk to combine.

When you have a white, glossy, grain-free meringue mixture, dab a few spots of it under each corner of the greaseproof paper to stop it flapping about in the oven and ruining the shape of your meringues. Follow the instructions on the next page for baking different types of meringue. With each different kind, once the baking time is up, turn the oven off and allow the meringues to cool in the oven.   >

< FOR MESSY MERINGUE MOUNDS

Scoop up apple-sized blobs with a big spoon and use another spoon to scrape the blob onto the baking sheet. You can do this really messily or fairly neatly, it's up to you. Bake for 2 hours, then turn the oven off and allow the meringues to cool slowly in the oven for 30 minutes. You can check that they are fully cooked by peeling one off the greaseproof paper – if it comes away cleanly, the meringues are ready.

FOR 'POOPS'

Transfer the mixture to a piping bag fitted with a large round nozzle and squeeze neat little kisses onto the baking sheet. It's best to start squeezing about 1cm/½in away from the surface to ensure you get chubby-bottomed poops. Pull away and stop squeezing once you have a poop about 5cm/2in high, to create that little point. Bake for 1 hour (if you have made much smaller mini-poops, these will only need about 30 minutes), then turn the oven off and let the poops cool slowly in the oven for 30 minutes. Peel one off the greaseproof paper to check that they are done – if it comes away cleanly, you're good to go. For tips, head to the QR code on page 24.

TEAM TIPS

If you want to colour your meringues, there are a couple of ways you can do it:

The natural way, using freeze-dried fruit powder: A couple of tablespoons of raspberry powder added at the end and mixed through creates a lovely soft pink colour, for example.

The not-so-natural way, using food colouring: Use colour gel or paste (not oil-based colour) and mix it into a couple of tablespoons of the meringue mixture in a small bowl to create a concentrated paste that you can then whisk or fold back into the rest of the meringue to achieve a smooth, all-over colour.

The stripy way: Before putting the white meringue mixture into a piping bag for 'pooping', use a small artist's paintbrush to brush gel or paste food colouring, loosened with a little water, up the insides of the piping bag. Bear in mind that this is super-concentrated stuff, so a little goes a long way! As you squeeze out the meringue, it will draw down the colour onto its sides, creating a pretty, stripy effect. To see this in action, head to the QR code on page 24.

**Makes enough for
1 batch of cupcakes
or to decorate a
20cm/8in cake**

100g egg whites
235g caster sugar
20g liquid glucose

80g water
a pinch of sea salt
½ tsp vanilla extract

ITALIAN MERINGUE

If you like toasted marshmallows, you'll love Italian meringue. It's a billowy, voluptuous meringue that is totally transformed when you give it a good seeing-to with a blowtorch. You can use it as it is, or toasted for that marshmallowy, slightly caramelised, campfire vibe.

First, ensure all of your equipment is completely free of grease by wiping it with vinegar or lemon juice and paper towels. Grease prevents egg whites from working their magic, so if you find you struggle to get lovely glossy white meringue, you might have grease on your bits and bobs.

Measure the egg whites into the bowl of a stand mixer fitted with the balloon whisk attachment. If you don't have a stand mixer, I recommend a large metal or glass bowl and at least an electric hand whisk, otherwise this will be a lot harder than it needs to be!

Attach a sugar thermometer to the inside of a saucepan, add the sugar, glucose and water and bring to the boil over a medium heat. Keep a close eye on the thermometer.

When the sugar mixture reaches 112–114°C, it's time to start whisking the egg whites, slowly at first, then increasing the speed until your eggs form soft peaks.

Meanwhile, when the sugar mixture has reached 118°C, remove it from the heat. With the stand mixer on a low-medium speed, very carefully and slowly pour in the sugar mixture. Try to pour it in a steady stream down the side of the bowl, as close to the top of the mixture as possible and not onto the whisk itself, otherwise all of the sugar will stick to the bowl rather than incorporate into the meringue.

When all of the sugar has been added, increase the speed and whisk until the meringue is completely cool.

Finally, whisk in the salt and the vanilla. It's now ready to use as directed in your recipe.

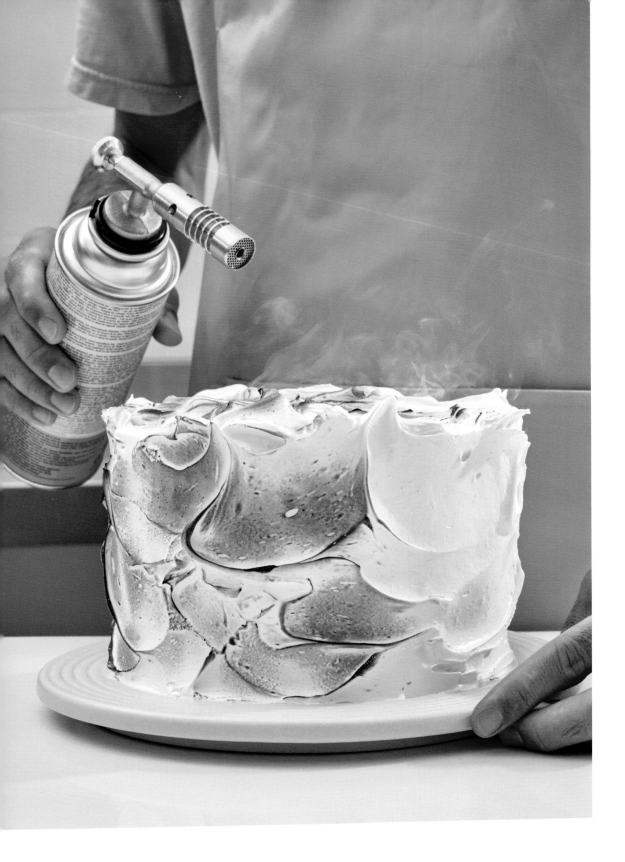

Makes 325g of Crème Pât and 735g of Crème Mousseline, enough to decorate 12 cupcakes

CRÈME PÂTISSIÈRE
225g milk
1 tsp vanilla extract

70g caster sugar
20g cornflour
1 egg plus 1 egg yolk

CRÈME MOUSSELINE
as left, plus:
a pinch of sea salt
115g unsalted butter, softened

CRÈME PÂTISSIÈRE & CRÈME MOUSSELINE

When it comes to custard, crème pât is the real deal! A thick, smooth custard, which is perfect for filling cakes and cupcakes. Whip it up with some soft butter and it becomes crème mousseline, a light whippy custard buttercream, perfect for toppings and decorating.

FOR THE CRÈME PÂTISSIÈRE
Heat the milk and vanilla in a small saucepan over a medium heat until it begins to steam.

Meanwhile, whisk together the sugar, cornflour, egg and egg yolk in a bowl until pale and thick.

Remove the hot milk from the heat and pour a ladleful into the egg mixture, whisking as you go. This is to 'temper' the eggs and prevent them from scrambling. Repeat this once or twice to make the egg mixture a bit warmer, then pour all of the egg mixture back into the saucepan and give it a stir.

Return the pan to a low-medium heat and cook for around 5 minutes until the custard is nice and thick, stirring constantly with a whisk to ensure it cooks evenly and doesn't catch on the bottom. You can test its thickness by coating the back of a wooden spoon and drawing a line in it with your finger. If the line remains in the custard, it's ready!

Remove from the heat and transfer to a bowl. Cover with clingfilm, making sure the film makes contact with the surface of the custard to prevent a skin forming, then leave to cool before putting it into the fridge to chill completely.

FOR CRÈME MOUSSELINE
If you have just made the crème pât, wait for it to reach room temperature before turning it into mousseline. If you have made it in advance and it has been in the fridge, let it come to room temperature, then transfer it to the bowl of a stand mixer fitted with the balloon whisk, or a large mixing bowl, and begin whisking on a medium-high speed. When it has been whisking for a minute or two, add the salt. With the whisk running, add little nuggets of the butter, one at a time. This will take a few minutes and you should end up with a silky, whippy, smooth and spreadable custard, which you can use to fill cakes, ice cupcakes and so much more.

TEAM TIP
If you've started making crème mousseline with crème pât that is still a bit on the chilly side, you might find that the mixture splits and looks as though it has curdled a bit. If this happens, just give it time. Crank up the speed on the mixer and keep it going. It will come together in no time.

BASIC GANACHES

Each makes enough to top a 20cm/8in square traybake with a 5mm/¼in layer of ganache; the Drip Ganache will drip and flood the top of a 20cm/8in cake

DARK CHOCOLATE GANACHE
150g dark chocolate chips (70% or 54% cocoa solids)
150g double cream

MILK CHOCOLATE GANACHE
200g milk chocolate chips
100g double cream

WHITE CHOCOLATE GANACHE
225g white chocolate chips
75g double cream

DARK CHOCOLATE DRIP GANACHE
80g dark chocolate chips (70% or 54% cocoa solids)
80g double cream

BUTTERY GANACHE ICING

Makes enough to decorate the top and sides of a 4-layer, 20cm/8in round cake; double the quantity to fill layers as well

300g dark chocolate
150g unsalted butter
150g double cream

CHOCOLATE GANACHE

Rich, chocolatey and utterly delicious, ganache is a true Crumbs & Doilies BFF. A blend of some of the most indulgent ingredients going, we use it to drip, fill, ice and decorate bakes. It can be smooth and runny, whipped and moussey, soft and spreadable or set and truffley. These are our go-to recipes for dark, milk and white chocolate ganache, plus a ganache drip and a Buttery Ganache Icing which we use to decorate some of our layer cakes.

FOR BASIC GANACHE
There are two ways to make this:

ON THE HOB
Place the chocolate in a heatproof bowl. In a small saucepan, heat the cream over a low–medium heat until it is steaming but not boiling, then pour the hot cream over the chocolate and let sit without stirring for about 1 minute. After this time, the cream will have melted the chocolate and you will be able to stir the two together to become one smooth, silky ganache.

IN A MICROWAVE
Put the chocolate and cream in a heat-proof bowl and heat in 15-second bursts, stirring gently after each go. After a few rounds, the chocolate will begin to melt and you can begin to combine the mixture by stirring with a small spatula. To avoid overheating the ganache and causing it to split, stop microwaving when there are still some nuggets of chocolate visible and use the residual heat to melt them as you stir.

FOR BUTTERY GANACHE ICING
Melt the chocolate and butter together in a small bowl, either over a bain-marie or in the microwave in 15-second bursts, stirring in between. Remove from the heat and pour in the cream, stirring with a spatula until combined. Leave to cool at room temperature, stirring every 10 minutes until it is a spreadable consistency. It is now ready to be spread all over your cake. You can also use it to crumb-coat your cake first, for maximum smoothness.

TEAM TIP
It is always best to make your ganache close to when you need it, as it will set firm over time, and warming it up to loosen it can cause the ganache to split.

Makes about 300g

300g good-quality white chocolate chips (look for something with 28% cocoa solids or more)

CARAMELISED WHITE CHOCOLATE

Cooking good-quality white chocolate slowly and gently doesn't actually caramelise anything. What happens is something called the Maillard reaction, which refers to the milk solids browning. But who cares that the name isn't strictly correct? What occurs is a total metamorphosis of white chocolate, from overly sweet and characterless to a gloriously warm, nutty, richly coloured elixir of joy for your bakes and your tastebuds. Make a batch, or double batch, and keep it in your fridge to use for a multitude of bakes, or just to nibble on.

There are two reliable ways to make this at home:

———

Line a 20cm/8in square baking tin with baking paper and set aside for now.

IN THE OVEN
Preheat your oven to 140°C (120°C fan). Spread the white chocolate evenly over a separate baking tray with a lip, then bake for 45–60 minutes, removing from the oven every 10 minutes to stir the chocolate around with a spatula. At first, not much will happen, then after a couple of rounds in the oven it will begin to seize up and become a thick paste. Don't panic, it's totally normal. Eventually, after you have repeated this process a few times, the white chocolate will melt and begin to turn a rich warm tan colour.

When you are happy with the colour (it should look like strong builder's tea or an over-zealous fake tan), remove from the oven and scrape every last bit into your prepared square tin. Leave to cool before putting it into the fridge to set completely.

I like to chop it into really chunky cubes so that I can eat it straight out of the fridge or use it in one of the many recipes in this book that calls for it.

IN THE MICROWAVE
In a heatproof bowl, melt the chocolate chips in a microwave on full power for 1 minute. Give them a stir with a heatproof spatula, then return the bowl to the microwave and keep heating, this time in 30-second bursts, stirring well in between. The chocolate will begin to thicken and seize, but keep going! Stir it thoroughly after each blast and after about 15–20 minutes it will have returned to a smooth, liquid consistency and turned a rich, warm tan colour not unlike Biscoff biscuit spread.

Follow the process described above for cooling, storing and nibbling.

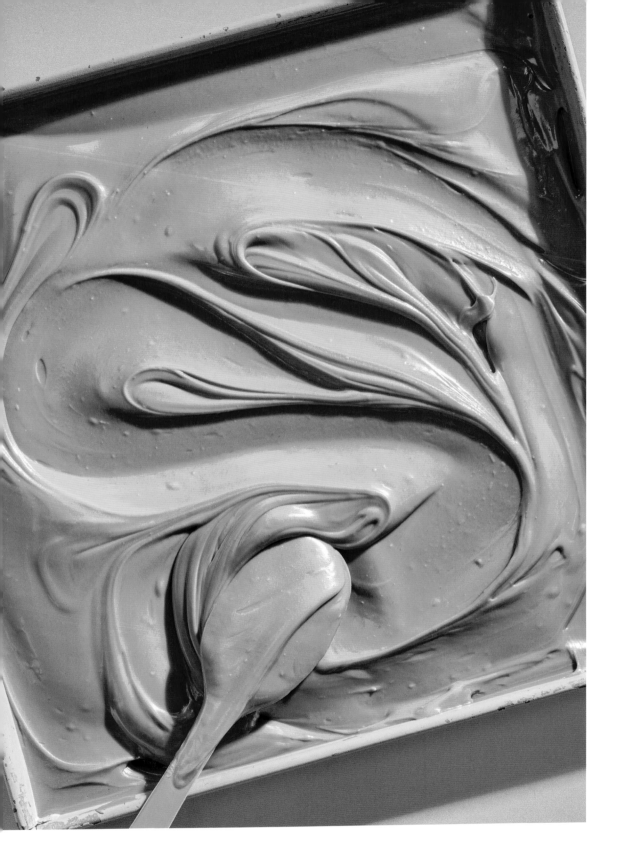

Makes about 200g

250g unsalted butter
(nope, nothing else)

BURNT BUTTER

Burnt butter (beurre noisette, if you're being fancy) transforms the flavour of your bakes when you substitute it for some or all of the butter in a recipe. It brings a pleasing nuttiness that adds such depth and richness that you'll be sticking it in just about everything once you've given it a go. Use it in its liquid form for blondies and cookies, or soft and spreadable for cakes and cupcakes. Just remember that when you make it you'll be cooking off most of the water in the butter and this can reduce the weight by as much as 20%, so always start with a little more butter to get the amount of burnt butter you need.

Melt the butter in a saucepan over a medium heat, stirring with a rubber spatula until the colour changes to a light amber and you can see little dark flecks forming on the bottom of the pan.

These are the milk solids that have gone through the Maillard reaction (commonly mistaken for caramelisation, which only really applies to the process of heating sugar). Remove from the heat before the flecks blacken completely.

Pour into a heatproof bowl or tray and leave to cool to room temperature, then refrigerate.

Bring back to room temperature to use in recipes for cake and buttercream, or melt again as per the recipe instructions.

Basics & BFFs

Makes 215g
(enough for 1 batch
of cupcakes)

50g unsalted butter,
   cold and cubed
zest of 1 lemon
65g lemon juice

65g caster sugar
1 egg
3 egg yolks

LEMON CURD

Lemon curd holds a special place in my heart. My grandma used to make a mean lemon curd sponge cake when we'd visit her as children, and when I first launched the Cupcake Jemma channel the cake was one of the very first recipes I shared. We use it so often in the bakery because it adds such a punchy zingyness to cakes and bakes.

———

Get your butter ready and put it into the fridge to keep cold.

Bring a small amount of water to a simmer in a small saucepan over a medium heat. This is for your bain-marie.

Combine the lemon zest, juice and sugar in a heatproof bowl. Add the egg and egg yolks and stir with a whisk before setting it over the pan of simmering water. Stir constantly with the whisk for 8–10 minutes. Eventually the mixture will begin to thicken as the eggs cook. You'll know it's ready when a dollop of curd dropped onto the surface remains there for a second or two.

Remove the bowl from the heat, grab your cold butter from the fridge and stir it into the curd with the whisk. This will stop it from cooking further but also help it to thicken even more as it cools, not to mention give the curd its distinctive buttery flavour.

Pass the still-warm curd through a sieve into a bowl to get rid of any zest and eggy bits, cover with clingfilm and pop into the fridge to chill completely. It will keep for 3–4 days in the fridge in an airtight container.

VARIATIONS
You can use this method with most citrus fruits or fruit with a lot of sharpness to them, such as **passion fruit**, **lime** or **yuzu**. Just replace the lemon juice in the recipe for the same amount of juice or pulp from your chosen fruit. Be wary of grapefruit, as the zest can make your mouth feel numb.

**Makes 260g
(enough for 1 batch
of cupcakes)**

400g frozen or fresh
   berries (raspberries,
   blueberries, strawberries,
   forest fruit mixes and
   cherries work well)

125g caster sugar

GOO

Goo is a steadfast Crumbs & Doilies BFF.
We use so much of it we had to purchase a
special machine to sieve out the millions of
seeds. He's called Augustus Goop! A little
looser and more intense than store-bought
jam, we use goo to fill cakes and cupcakes,
flavour buttercreams and to ripple through
sponges. Goo can be stored in an airtight
container for up to a week, so you can get
really prepared!

———

Tumble the berries into a saucepan and
add the sugar. Over a medium heat, melt
down the fruit and cook until bubbling,
stirring occasionally, then reduce the heat
to low and simmer for 20–40 minutes (the
time depends on the type of fruit and how
thick you want your goo to be). Make sure
you give it a stir every now and then to
make sure it doesn't catch and burn on the
bottom of the saucepan. If it looks as though
it's headed in this direction, reduce the
heat further.

When it's a loose jammy consistency, take
your goo off the heat. While it is still warm,
push through a fine sieve to get rid of any
lumpy pulp or seeds. Sometimes, the sieving
process reveals that you haven't actually
achieved 'peak goo', especially for fruits with
a lot of seeds, such as raspberries. In this
case, return the sieved goo to a saucepan
and reduce a bit more over a low heat.

Leave to cool before transferring it to
an airtight container. Refrigerate until you
need it. Goo will keep in the fridge for
up to a week.

———

TEAM TIP
Some fruit takes a bit more effort to
become goo-worthy. Strawberries, for
example, might need help to break down
with a little squash from a potato masher.
To bring out more flavour in the fruit, you
can add a squeeze of lemon juice – add
a little at a time and taste as you go.

Makes about 250g

250g nuts (peanuts, hazelnuts and pistachios work brilliantly)

a pinch of sea salt or sugar (optional)

NUT BUTTER

If you struggle to find certain nut butters (such as pistachio) in your local area, why not make your own to include in your bakes? It feels crazy to call this a 'recipe' because it's so blooming easy, provided you have a blender or food processor. If you don't, you might struggle to achieve the right consistency.

———

Preheat your oven to 190°C (170°C fan).

Spread the nuts over one or two baking trays and roast them in the oven for 5–8 minutes, then remove.

If your chosen nuts have skins on them, such as hazelnuts, you'll want to remove as much as you can before you put them in the blender. The best way to do this is to tip the warm nuts into the middle of a clean tea towel, gather up the corners to create a little bag, then use your other hand to rub and squish the nuts against each other. The skins will come away from the nuts and stop the nut butter from taking on their bitter flavour.

Let the nuts cool so that they're slightly warm, then tip them into a food processor and blitz for 10-15 minutes. The change the nuts go through is really interesting. Everything starts off really dry, then clumpy and crumbly, then as more of the oils are released it almost liquefies, becoming a smooth, sometimes runny, paste that you can use wherever a recipe asks for a nut butter or paste.

Add salt or even sugar if you like, to season. Nut butter will keep for up to 4 weeks in an airtight container in the fridge, or up to 1 week at room temperature.

Makes a generous quantity

PLAIN PIE CRUMB
110g plain flour
20g caster sugar
a pinch of sea salt
60g unsalted butter, melted
1 tsp cold water

For Matcha Pie Crumb:
add ½ tsp matcha green tea powder

CRUMBLE PIE CRUMB
80g plain flour
20g rolled/porridge oats
10g caster sugar
10g demerara sugar
a pinch of sea salt
40g unsalted butter, melted

CHOCOLATE PIE CRUMB
60g plain flour
50g cocoa powder
60g caster sugar
a pinch of sea salt

20g unsalted butter, melted
20g vegetable oil
½ tsp vanilla extract
1 tsp cold water

BIRTHDAY CAKE PIE CRUMB
110g plain flour
a large pinch of sea salt
20g caster sugar
10g light brown sugar
40g unsalted butter, melted

15g vegetable oil
½ tsp vanilla extract
1–2 tsp cold water

CINNAMON PIE CRUMB
110g plain flour
a pinch of sea salt
10g caster sugar
10g demerara sugar
1 tsp ground cinnamon
60g unsalted butter, melted
1 tsp cold water

PIE CRUMB

These little nuggets of deliciousness have gone through a few improvements since we first began making them at C&D and I consider them to be one of the most fun things to make in the bakery, as well as one of the hardest things to resist once they're baked. Pie crumb is surprisingly versatile and, as you can see here, can be made in loads of different flavours. It'll add texture, flavour and pie vibes to bakes such as the Lemon Mess Cake (page 242), Cake Batter Cupcakes (page 84) and Apple Crumble NY Cookies (page 192). This makes more than enough for sprinkling on one batch of cupcakes or one cake. So, you could just make half the quantity, but we guarantee you that you will be munching on these as you bake, so by making more we are doing you a favour...

Preheat your oven to 190°C (170°C fan) and line a baking tray with greaseproof paper.

Mix all of the ingredients for your chosen pie crumb together in a bowl using a wooden spoon. When it is starting to clump together into big lumps of dough, assess whether it looks too wet or too dry. Too wet and you should add 10g extra flour; too dry, add a little more water.

Now get your hands in there. The trick to getting lovely nuggets is to start by sprinkling the mixture gently through your fingers to break up the lumps. It's difficult to explain this next technique but my best effort is to tell you to claw the mixture by making a 'comb' with each set of fingers, scooping down the slides of the bowl and under the nuggets then allowing them to fall through your fingers. I do this quite a few times, breaking up any large nuggets individually so that you end up with some good, smooth, round nuggets of various sizes, from pea-sized to sprinkle-sized, a little bit like soil!

Scatter the nuggets evenly across the baking tray, then bake for 10–12 minutes until golden and no longer doughy. You might want to give them a shuffle around halfway to break them up and make sure they cook evenly.

Leave to cool completely before putting your pie crumb into an airtight container, ready to use on your bakes. It will keep for a couple of weeks at room temperature.

Makes around 800g, which is enough to make and decorate an entire Cookie Dough Cake (page 257), or the tops of your cakes and cupcakes with lots left over for emergencies

240g unsalted butter, softened
200g plain flour, plus extra for dusting

140g caster sugar
90g soft light brown sugar
1 tsp sea salt

1 tsp vanilla extract
4 tbsp plain yoghurt
100g dark chocolate chips (54% cocoa solids)

COOKIE DOUGH

Ahh, cookie dough. Who hasn't had a nibble on the stuff while preparing a batch of cookies? Our recipe is perfect to use as a filling and a topping for so many bakes and desserts, and the best thing is it's perfectly safe to eat in it's raw form, provided you prepare the flour properly to kill off any bacteria that might upset your tummy.

———

Grease and line a small deep dish or baking tray (about 16 x 20cm/6 x 8in) with greaseproof paper and dust it lightly with flour to prevent the cookie dough from sticking. Preheat your oven to 190°C (170°C fan) and line a separate baking tray with greaseproof paper.

Spread the flour evenly over the baking tray and bake for 10 minutes, stirring halfway, to kill any bacteria that might be lurking in the raw flour. Leave to cool completely.

Place all the ingredients, except the chocolate chips, into a bowl and beat together well until light in colour (with an electric hand mixer this should take about 30 seconds), then gently mix in the chocolate chips.

Tip the cookie dough into your lined tray and spread it out with a palette knife. Aim for the slab of dough to be about 2.5cm/1in thick, so that when you chop it you get nice chunks. Put the tray into the freezer.

When you need the cookie dough, remove from the freezer and chop it into pieces.

———

TEAM TIP
Cookie dough will keep for up to 6 weeks in the freezer. Just wrap it up well or put it into a ziplock bag or airtight container.

Makes enough to make the OG Cornflake Crunch (page 148) and decorate the Cereal Milk Cupcakes (page 74) with plenty left to nibble on and you WILL want to nibble on these

30g malted milk powder (such as Horlicks)
30g caster sugar
a pinch of sea salt

75g unsalted butter, melted
120g plain cornflakes

MALTY CORNFLAKES

Beware! These cornflakes are almost impossible to resist. Once I break the seal, that's it. Many times, I have found my hand wrist-deep in the stuff, pulling them out by the fistful, when I only meant to go in for a little nibble! We use Malty Cornflakes for brownies, bakes, on top of cakes, inside cakes, almost anywhere in fact! The crispiness holds up really well, even sandwiched between two sponges and enrobed in buttercream, and will give your bakes some added crunch and flavour.

Preheat your oven to 170°C (150°C fan) and line two baking trays with greaseproof paper.

Combine the malted milk powder, sugar and salt in a small bowl and give it a good stir.

In a separate large bowl, pour the melted butter over the cornflakes and toss them all around so that they are all covered in butter. Sprinkle over the dry ingredients and stir everything well so that every cornflake is covered in a malty, sugary, buttery coating.

Scatter and spread the mixture out across the baking trays, separating the cornflakes as much as possible. Bake for 10 minutes.

Leave to cool, then break up any large cornflakey masses and store in an airtight container, ready to use in all manner of delicious ways (if you can resist eating them all as they are, of course!).

CUPCAKES

CUPCAKES

We've come a long way since the early days when I only sold simple vanilla-, chocolate- and lemon-flavoured cupcakes on my market stall! My passion for baking and creating led me down a rabbit hole of wild and wonderful flavour combinations, and we've become known all over the world for our cupcakes (I'm not called Cupcake Jemma for nothing!). The bakers at Crumbs & Doilies are always experimenting with new flavours and this chapter is filled with some of the best we've ever made!

We use an all-in-one method to make our cupcake sponges, which relies on the raising agent to lift the cake, rather than whipping the ingredients. This produces a light, moist sponge that doesn't dry out as quickly as one made using the more traditional creaming method (we use that for bigger cakes that can take the extra air). It's also super speedy, meaning cupcakes are a great option if you need to whip up something quickly. You can make cupcakes really pure and simple, or lavish them with time, effort and lots of different elements to make them really special.

There are also many ways you can decorate cupcakes and to get you started, here are a couple of QR codes that you can refer to for the basics of cupcake decorating.

Filling cupcake cases

Filling a cupcake

Piping a cupcake

CEREAL MILK CUPCAKES 74

CHOCOLATE INSANITY CUPCAKES 76

RHUBARB & CUSTARD CUPCAKES 78

TAHINI & CHOCOLATE CUPCAKES 80

RASPBERRY BOMBE CUPCAKES 82

CAKE BATTER CUPCAKES 84

BAKLAVA CUPCAKES 86

FERRERO ROCHER CUPCAKES 88

KEY LIME PIE CUPCAKES 90

MISO CARAMEL CUPCAKES 92

BREAKFAST BOWL CUPCAKES 95

APPLE PIE CUPCAKES 98

SALTED CARAMEL PRETZEL CUPCAKES 101

BLACKBERRY APPLE CRUMBLE CUPCAKES 104

BLACK SESAME & WHITE CHOCOLATE CUPCAKES 107

STRAWBERRY SHORTCAKE CUPCAKES 110

HIBISCUS & LIME CUPCAKES 113

ROASTED STRAWBERRY & YUZU CUPCAKES 116

MILK CHOCOLATE PASSION FRUIT CUPCAKES 119

BANANARAMA CUPCAKES 122

BLACK FOREST CUPCAKES 125

Makes 12

PREP
1 x batch of Malty
Cornflakes (page 68)

CEREAL MILK
50g cornflakes
20g soft light
brown sugar

400ml milk
a pinch of sea salt

CEREAL MILK SPONGE
125g self-raising flour
¼ tsp bicarbonate
of soda
⅛ tsp sea salt
125g caster sugar

125g unsalted butter,
softened
2 eggs
2 tbsp Cereal Milk
(see left)

**CEREAL MILK
BUTTERCREAM**
285g unsalted
butter, softened

¼ tsp sea salt
¼ tsp malted milk
powder (such as
Horlicks)
450g icing sugar, sifted
1½ tbsp Cereal Milk
(see left)

TO FINISH
rainbow sprinkles

CEREAL MILK CUPCAKES

If you go to New York, you must try the famous Cereal Milk soft-serve from Milk Bar. Christina Tosi, the iconic bake-shop's founder, is an inspiration to many, including us, so we had to pay tribute to this epic dessert by cupcakifying it! Reminiscent of the milk left at the bottom of the bowl after you've eaten all the cereal, the cereal milk flavour is subtle but so evocative.

———

Make the Malty Cornflakes as directed on page 68 and set aside for later.

FOR THE CEREAL MILK
Preheat your oven to 160°C (140°C fan). Spread the cornflakes evenly over a baking sheet and bake for 15 minutes.

Put the still-hot cornflakes into a saucepan along with the sugar, milk and salt. Bring to the boil, then reduce to a low simmer and cook for a couple of minutes. Leave to cool in the pan for 5 minutes, then strain out the cornflakes and set the liquid aside to cool.

FOR THE CEREAL MILK SPONGE
Increase the oven to 190°C (170°C fan) and line a 12-hole cupcake tin with paper cases.

In the bowl of a stand mixer fitted with the

paddle attachment, or a mixing bowl, sift together the flour, bicarb, salt and sugar. Add the butter and eggs and beat on a slow speed, increasing to medium and mixing for 30 seconds (longer by hand) until well combined. Add the cereal milk and beat for 30 seconds, scraping the sides and bottom of the bowl so you don't miss any bits. You should have a smooth batter with no lumps.

Distribute the batter evenly among the paper cases until they are three-quarters full. Bake for 18–20 minutes until the tops spring back when pressed. Leave to cool.

FOR THE CEREAL MILK BUTTERCREAM
In the bowl of a stand mixer fitted with the paddle attachment, or a mixing bowl, beat the butter, salt and malt powder together for 5 minutes until really pale and whippy. Add the icing sugar in two stages, beating vigorously for 3–5 minutes after each addition. Add the cereal milk a little at a time, beating for 3–5 minutes until you have a spreadable buttercream that holds its shape.

TO FINISH
Fill a piping bag with a star-shaped nozzle with the buttercream, then pipe neat swirls on top of your cupcakes. Finish with the malty cornflakes and colourful sprinkles.

Cupcakes

Makes 12

PREP
1 x batch of Chocolate
Cream Cheese Icing
(page 38)

CHOCOLATE TRUFFLES
150g dark chocolate
chips (54% cocoa solids)

15g unsalted butter
60g double cream
25g cocoa powder

CHOCOLATE MUDCAKES
100g unsalted butter
50ml brewed coffee
(or 50ml hot water with
2 tsp instant coffee
granules)

125g dark chocolate
(70% cocoa solids)
75g buttermilk
45g vegetable oil
2 eggs
215g caster sugar
150g plain flour
30g cocoa powder
¼ tsp bicarbonate of soda
¼ tsp sea salt

**CHOCOLATE SAUCE
FILLING**
60g double cream
25g caster sugar
a pinch of sea salt
100g golden syrup
30g dark chocolate chips
20g cocoa powder

CHOCOLATE INSANITY CUPCAKES

How much chocolate is too much chocolate? Let's find out! This cupcake is über chocolatey, rich, fudgy and indulgent, and we think it's just right for all the chocolate lovers out there.

———

Prepare your Chocolate Cream Cheese Icing as directed on page 38 and set aside.

FOR THE CHOCOLATE TRUFFLES
Melt the chocolate and butter, either over a bain-marie or in the microwave in 15-second bursts, then add the cream and stir to combine. Cool to a spreadable consistency, then place in a piping bag fitted with a large round nozzle. Line a baking sheet with greaseproof paper. Pipe thick sausages of the ganache onto the paper and refrigerate for at least 30 minutes.

Sift the cocoa into a bowl. Slice the chilled ganache into 4cm/1½in pieces, then toss in the cocoa to cover. Refrigerate until needed (make sure they aren't touching each other).

FOR THE CHOCOLATE MUDCAKES
Preheat your oven to 190°C (170°C fan) and line a 12-hole cupcake tin with paper cases.

In a small saucepan over a low heat, melt the butter, coffee and chocolate, stirring constantly. Leave to cool slightly.

Whisk together the buttermilk, oil and eggs in a large bowl. Pour in the cooled chocolate mixture and whisk to combine.

In a separate bowl, whisk together the sugar, flour, cocoa, bicarb and salt, then add to the wet ingredients and whisk to combine.

Distribute the batter evenly among the paper cases until they are three-quarters full. Bake for 18–20 minutes until an inserted skewer comes out clean. Leave to cool.

FOR THE CHOCOLATE SAUCE FILLING
Bring the cream, sugar, salt and golden syrup to the boil in a small saucepan.

Combine the chocolate and cocoa in a bowl. Pour the hot mixture over and let it sit for a minute, then stir to combine. Cool for 5 minutes, then pour into a piping bag.

TO FINISH
Using an apple corer, remove the middles of the cupcakes. Fill the holes with roughly half of the chocolate sauce. Using a piping bag fitted with a star nozzle, pipe swirls of chocolate cream cheese icing on top of each cake. Drizzle with more chocolate sauce and finish with a chocolate truffle.

Cupcakes

Makes 12

PREP
1 x batch of Crème
Mousseline (page 50)
1 x batch of Crumble Pie
Crumb (page 64)

RHUBARB GOO FILLING
300g rhubarb, chopped
3 tbsp caster sugar
zest of 1 orange
1 vanilla pod, split

RHUBARB AND VANILLA SPONGE
125g self-raising flour
125g caster sugar
¼ tsp bicarbonate of soda
125g unsalted butter,
softened

2 eggs
1½ tbsp milk
½ tsp vanilla extract
3–4 tbsp Rhubarb
Goo Filling (see left)

RHUBARB & CUSTARD CUPCAKES

Another dessert-to-cake mash-up that I almost prefer to the original dessert! Rhubarb and custard is a truly British flavour combo, which pairs the sharpness of fresh rhubarb with the sweet, comforting notes of vanilla. This cupcake is topped with one of my favourite things of all time: crème mousseline. If you've not made it before, it's essentially custard buttercream (you're welcome!). Top it off with some crumble pie crumb for those classic pudding vibes.

———

Make the Crème Mousseline (page 50) and Pie Crumb (page 64), then set aside.

FOR THE RHUBARB GOO FILLING
Preheat your oven to 190°C (170°C fan).

Combine all the ingredients in a roasting tin and toss well. Spread the rhubarb out evenly and bake for 10–15 minutes, then remove from the oven and strain the roasted rhubarb through a sieve set over a bowl or jug to catch the sweet, pink rhubarb syrup.

Put the rhubarb pulp into a blender and whizz until smooth, then cool completely. This is your 'goo'.

Pour the rhubarb syrup into a small pan and simmer over a low heat until reduced by half. Leave to cool and set aside.

FOR THE RHUBARB SPONGE
Line a 12-hole cupcake tin with paper cases.

In a stand mixer fitted with the paddle attachment, or a mixing bowl, sift together the flour, sugar and bicarb. Add the butter and eggs and beat for 30 seconds until well combined. Add the milk and vanilla, and beat to a smooth batter, scraping any stray bits from the sides of the bowl as you go.

Dollop 2 tablespoons of the goo on top of the batter and slightly swirl it through as you distribute the batter evenly among the paper cases. Try not to mix the goo in too much – you want it to be a 'ripple'. Add more goo if you run out as you scoop, ensuring you keep enough to fill the cupcakes with later on.

Bake for 18–20 minutes until the tops spring back when pressed. Leave to cool.

TO FINISH
Remove the centre of each cupcake with an apple corer. Fill a piping bag with the remaining rhubarb goo and fill each cupcake, being careful not to overfill.

Put the crème mousseline into a large piping bag fitted with a big star nozzle and pipe swirls on top of each cupcake. Drizzle with the rhubarb syrup, then finish with a cluster of crumble pie crumb nuggets.

Cupcakes

Makes 12

SESAME BRITTLE
110g caster sugar
2 tbsp water
15g unsalted butter
½ tsp vanilla extract
a pinch of sea salt
15g white sesame seeds

15g black sesame seeds
20g each of white and
  dark chocolate, melted
  (optional)

TAHINI SPONGE
125g unsalted butter,
  softened
125g self-raising flour

125g caster sugar
¼ tsp bicarbonate
  of soda
a pinch of sea salt
2 eggs
25g tahini
1 tbsp whole milk

**TAHINI & CHOCOLATE
SWISS MERINGUE
BUTTERCREAMS**
1 x batch of Swiss
  Meringue Buttercream
  (page 40)
60g tahini
150g dark chocolate,
  melted and cooled
  slightly

TAHINI & CHOCOLATE CUPCAKES

If you're baking for someone who hasn't got a sweet tooth, this cupcake is your guy! Smooth, with a subtle nuttiness, tahini brings a pleasing warm flavour and balances out the sweetness of the chocolate. Even the sesame brittle has a lovely sweet and bitter thing going on.

FOR THE SESAME BRITTLE
Line a baking sheet with greaseproof paper or a silpat.

Put the sugar and water into a small saucepan and stir a little to ensure the sugar is soaked. Place over a medium heat and bring to the boil, without stirring. Continue to cook, making sure you keep an eye on it. Do not stir! This can cause it to crystallise. When the sugar has turned a light amber colour, remove from the heat and stir in the butter, vanilla, salt and three-quarters of the sesame seeds. Stir quickly and thoroughly, then pour the mixture onto the baking sheet, sprinkle with the remaining sesame seeds and leave to cool down completely.

Once cool, break the brittle up into large shards. If you want to be fancy, like us, drizzle some melted chocolate across each shard in a zigzag to jazz it up even further.

FOR THE TAHINI SPONGE
Preheat your oven to 190°C (170°C fan) and line a 12-hole cupcake tin with paper cases.

Put the butter, flour, sugar, bicarb, salt, eggs and tahini into a stand mixer fitted with the paddle attachment, or a large mixing bowl, and beat for 30 seconds until thoroughly combined. Add the milk and beat for another 30 seconds, stopping to scrape down the sides of the bowl to catch any missed bits.

Distribute the batter evenly among the paper cases until they are three-quarters full. Bake for 18–20 minutes until the tops of the cakes are golden and springy. Leave to cool.

FOR THE BUTTERCREAMS
Make the Swiss Meringue Buttercream as directed on page 40. Remove a third of the mixture to a separate bowl and mix in the tahini. Mix the melted chocolate into the remaining buttercream.

TO FINISH
Fill two piping bags fitted with star nozzles with the buttercreams. Pipe a large swirl of chocolate buttercream on top of each cupcake and top with a smaller swirl of tahini buttercream. Finish with shards of the brittle.

Makes 12

PREP
1 x batch of Raspberry
 Goo (page 60)
1 x batch of French
 Meringues (page 45)

CHOCOLATE CUPCAKES
140g plain flour
185g caster sugar
35g cocoa powder
¼ tsp sea salt
½ tsp bicarbonate of soda

2 eggs
125g coffee, cold
125g buttermilk
105g vegetable oil
35g dark chocolate
 chips

RASPBERRY BUTTERCREAM
285g unsalted butter,
 softened
¼ tsp sea salt
450g icing sugar, sifted
3–5 tbsp Raspberry Goo
 (see Prep)

RASPBERRY BOMBE CUPCAKES

Raspberry Bombe has been on the Crumbs & Doilies menu for years, so there's no way it wasn't making the cut for the book. Raspberry and chocolate is one of those combinations that will always be in fashion. We've no idea why we called it a bombe – it's not frozen or spherical, like other desserts of the same name – but it does explode with flavour, so we're sticking with it!

Make the Raspberry Goo (page 60) and French Meringues (page 45) and set aside.

FOR THE CHOCOLATE CUPCAKES

Preheat your oven to 170°C (150°C fan) and line a 12-hole cupcake tin with paper cases.

In a medium mixing bowl, whisk together the flour, sugar, cocoa, salt and bicarb.

In a separate large mixing bowl, whisk together the eggs, coffee, buttermilk, oil and chocolate chips.

Tip the dry ingredients into the wet ingredients and whisk together until you have a batter that is smooth, aside from the chocolate chips.

Using a jug, distribute the batter among the paper cases until they are three-quarters full. Bake for 20–22 minutes until the tops are springy to the touch. Leave to cool.

FOR THE RASPBERRY BUTTERCREAM

In the bowl of a stand mixer fitted with the paddle attachment, or a mixing bowl, beat the butter and salt on a high speed for 5 minutes until the butter becomes pale, light and whippy. Add the sifted icing sugar in two stages, beating for 3–5 minutes on a high speed after each addition. Add the raspberry goo and beat again for a few minutes. If you feel that the buttercream could take more liquid, add more of the raspberry goo, one tablespoon at a time, so you don't add too much. You should have a light, floppy, pink buttercream.

TO FINISH

Remove the middle of each cupcake with an apple corer. Put the leftover raspberry goo into a piping bag and and use it to fill the cupcake holes, remembering to reserve some for decorating

Fill a large piping bag fitted with a star-shaped nozzle with the buttercream and pipe a nice fat swirl on the top of each cupcake. If your piping skills aren't up to much, don't panic – this is the cupcake that will conceal your inadequacies!

Drizzle some of the remaining raspberry goo over the top of the iced cupcakes, then crush up some meringues into messy pieces and scatter them all over the top so that you have a disorderly but enticing mess of a cupcake!

Cupcakes

Makes 12

PREP
1 x batch of Birthday
Cake Pie Crumb
(page 64)

FUNFETTI SPONGE
125g self-raising flour
100g caster sugar
25g light brown sugar
¼ tsp bicarbonate of soda
¼ tsp sea salt
125g unsalted butter,
  softened
75g white chocolate
  chips, finely chopped
30g rainbow sprinkles
2 eggs
1½ tbsp milk
½ tsp vanilla extract

**CAKE BATTER
BUTTERCREAM**
80g plain flour
285g unsalted butter,
  softened
¼ tsp sea salt
450g icing sugar, sifted
1½ tbsp milk
1 tsp vanilla extract
30g rainbow sprinkles

CAKE BATTER CUPCAKES

This cupcake is designed for all the spoon lickers out there and won't get you told off! The buttercream is made with flour, which gives it that unmistakable cake-batter flavour and texture. We cook the flour before adding it to the buttercream, which ensures any nasty bacteria that might be lurking in the flour are killed off. These are intensely vanilla-y and full of colourful sprinkles, just like a classic birthday cake should be.

———

Make the Birthday Cake Pie Crumb as directed on page 64 and set aside.

FOR THE FUNFETTI SPONGE
Preheat your oven to 190°C (170°C fan). Line a 12-hole cupcake tin with paper cases and line a baking sheet with greaseproof paper.

In the bowl of a stand mixer fitted with the paddle attachment, or a mixing bowl, sift together the flour, sugars, bicarb and salt. Add the butter, chocolate chips, sprinkles and eggs, and beat on medium speed for about 30 seconds until well combined.

Add the milk and vanilla and beat for another 30 seconds, stopping halfway to scrape down the sides and bottom of the bowl to make sure every last bit is included.

Distribute the batter evenly among the paper cases until they are three-quarters full. Bake for 18–20 minutes until the tops spring back when pressed. Leave to cool.

FOR THE CAKE BATTER BUTTERCREAM
Spread the flour over the baking sheet and bake for 10 minutes. Remove and leave to cool while you make the buttercream.

In the bowl of a stand mixer fitted with the paddle attachment, or a large mixing bowl, beat the butter and salt on a high speed for at least 5 minutes until super pale and fluffy. Add the icing sugar in two stages, beating for 3–5 minutes after each addition. Stop the mixer to add the flour, then mix on a high speed before adding the milk and vanilla. Go easy with the milk at first and add more if you feel the icing is too stiff. Beat on a high speed for 3–4 minutes. Stir the sprinkles through, then transfer the buttercream to a large piping bag fitted with a star nozzle.

TO FINISH
Pipe generous swirls of the buttercream onto each cupcake, then finish with a cluster of the birthday cake pie crumb on top.

Cupcakes

Makes 12

PREP
1 x batch of Pistachio Swiss Meringue Buttercream (page 40)

HONEY CARAMEL
80g caster sugar
90g water
130g honey
150g double cream

PISTACHIO SPONGE
125g self-raising flour
125g caster sugar
¼ tsp bicarbonate of soda
125g unsalted butter, softened
2 eggs

1½ tbsp milk
25g smooth pistachio paste (store-bought or see page 62)

TO FINISH
a small handful of chopped pistachios

BAKLAVA CUPCAKES

This is a firm favourite among the C&D team, with many citing it as their favourite flavour on the menu. It's our take on the classic sticky sweet pastry dessert and combines honey, pistachios and a whole lotta caramel.

———

Make the Pistachio Swiss Meringue Buttercream as directed on page 40 and set aside.

FOR THE HONEY CARAMEL
Put the sugar, water and honey into a medium pan with a sugar thermometer attached to the inside and stir to combine. Over a low–medium heat and without stirring, bring the mixture to the boil and let it simmer for about 10 minutes. This caramel bubbles up a lot, so keep an eye on it. If it looks as though it's creeping toward the top of the pan, remove from the heat for a few seconds to let the bubbles subside, then return it to the heat and carry on. When the temperature reaches 160–165°C, remove the pan from the heat and pour in the cream, a little at a time, stirring carefully and quickly. Beware of steam and hot bubbles! When the cream is completely combined, pour the caramel into a heatproof bowl and leave to cool down completely.

FOR THE PISTACHIO SPONGE
Preheat your oven to 190°C (170°C fan) and line a 12-hole cupcake tin with paper cases.

In the bowl of a stand mixer fitted with the paddle attachment, or a large mixing bowl, sift together the flour, sugar and bicarb. Add the butter, then the eggs, and beat on a medium–high speed for around 30 seconds. Add the milk and the pistachio paste and beat in for a further 30 seconds, stopping halfway to scrape the sides and bottom of the bowl.

Distribute the batter evenly among the paper cases until they are three-quarters full. Bake for 18–20 minutes, or until the cupcakes are nice and springy on the top. Leave to cool.

TO FINISH
Using an apple corer, remove the middles of the cupcakes (snack time!).

Fill a piping bag with the honey caramel and fill the holes in the cupcakes. Make sure you keep some back for drizzling the tops.

Fill a large piping bag fitted with a star-shaped nozzle with the pistachio buttercream and pipe generous swirls on top of each cupcake. Finish them off with a drizzle of the remaining honey caramel and a sprinkling of chopped pistachios.

Makes 12

HAZELNUT BUTTERCREAM
285g unsalted butter, softened
¼ tsp sea salt
450g icing sugar, sifted
4 tbsp Hazelnut Butter (page 62)
1½ tbsp milk

HAZELNUT SPONGE
115g self-raising flour
10g cocoa powder
a pinch of sea salt
¼ tsp bicarbonate of soda
115g caster sugar
10g soft light brown sugar
125g unsalted butter, softened

2 eggs
1½ tbsp milk
25g Hazelnut Butter (page 62)

FILLING
100ml double cream
1 tsp icing sugar, sifted
1 tbsp Hazelnut Butter (page 62)

TO FINISH
200g dark chocolate (50% cocoa solids), melted
½ tsp cocoa butter, melted
100g hazelnut nibs or chopped roasted hazelnuts

FERRERO ROCHER CUPCAKES

We all remember those naff Ferrero Rocher adverts from the '80s and '90s, but these cupcakes are anything but naff. Light chocolatey hazelnut sponge, filled with whipped hazelnut cream, topped with hazelnut buttercream, then dunked in chocolate and rolled in nuts. Perfect for the ambassador's reception, and anyone else who wants one!

Prepare the Hazelnut Buttercream as directed on page 36. Cover and set aside.

FOR THE HAZELNUT SPONGE
Preheat your oven to 190°C (170°C fan) and line a 12-hole cupcake tin with paper cases.

Sift the flour, cocoa, salt, bicarb and sugars into the bowl of a stand mixer fitted with the paddle attachment, or a large bowl. Add the butter and eggs, and beat on a medium–high speed for 30 seconds until well combined. Add the milk and hazelnut butter and beat for 30 seconds, stopping to scrape the sides and bottom halfway through, until you have a smooth batter.

Distribute the batter evenly among the paper cases until they are three-quarters full.

Bake for 18–20 minutes until the tops spring back when gently pressed. Leave to cool.

FOR THE FILLING
In a bowl, whip the cream, sugar and hazelnut butter with a balloon whisk until medium-soft peaks are forming, then put the mixture into a piping bag.

TO FINISH
Using an apple corer, remove the centre of each cupcake, then fill the holes with the cream filling. Take care not to overfill.

Put your buttercream into a piping bag fitted with a large round nozzle and squeeze a neat blob of buttercream on top of each cupcake.

Put the iced cupcakes in the fridge for 15 minutes while you melt the chocolate for the topping in a bain-marie or in the microwave in short bursts. Add the melted cocoa butter and stir to combine, then leave to cool for 5 minutes.

Dip the chilled iced cupcake tops into the chocolate, allowing the excess to dribble back into the bowl. Sprinkle with hazelnuts to finish.

Makes 12

PREP
1 batch of Lime Curd
(page 58)

BUTTERY BISCUIT BASE
90g digestive biscuits,
    crushed to a
    fine crumb
25g unsalted butter,
    melted
10g golden syrup

LIME SPONGE
125g self-raising flour
125g caster sugar
¼ tsp bicarbonate of
    soda
zest of 2 limes
125g unsalted butter,
    softened

2 eggs
1 tbsp whole milk
1 tbsp lime juice

TO FINISH
1 x batch of Italian
    Meringue (page 48)

KEY LIME PIE CUPCAKES

Traditionally made with Key limes (as the name suggests), the Key Lime Pie is a sharp, sweet, biscuit-encrusted, meringue-topped extravaganza. This cupcake is our sponge-based version and is one of my favourite flavours on the menu. Make it even more pie-like, if you fancy, with some Pie Crumb (page 64).

———

Make the Lime Curd in the same way as the Lemon Curd on page 58. Cover and set aside.

Preheat your oven to 190°C (170°C fan) and line a 12-hole cupcake tin with paper cases.

FOR THE BUTTERY BISCUIT BASE
In a bowl, mix all the ingredients thoroughly until the mixture resembles damp sand and keeps its shape when squeezed together. Scoop a tablespoon of the mixture into each of your paper cases and use the back of a spoon or a shot glass to press the crumbs firmly into a packed, even layer.

FOR THE LIME SPONGE
In the bowl of a stand mixer fitted with the paddle attachment, or a large mixing bowl, sift together the flour, sugar and bicarb. Zest the limes directly on top, then add the butter and eggs and beat on a medium–high speed for 30 seconds. Add the milk and lime juice and beat for another 30 seconds,

stopping halfway to scrape the sides and bottom of the bowl.

Distribute the batter evenly among the paper cases until they are three-quarters full, then bake for 18–20 minutes or until the tops spring back when pressed. Leave to cool.

TO FINISH
Prepare the Italian Meringue as directed on page 48, then put it into a large piping bag fitted with a round nozzle. Put your lime curd into a small piping bag.

Remove the centre of each cupcake using an apple corer, then pipe the lime curd into the holes.

Top the cupcakes with a neatly coiled mound of piped Italian meringue, then get your kitchen blowtorch out and give them a light toasting. If you don't have a blowtorch, place the cupcakes on a baking sheet and flash them briefly under a very hot grill until the tops are nice and toasty. But keep an eye on them, as this doesn't take long!

———

TEAM TIP
Zesting your lime directly over the batter mixture, rather than in a separate bowl, ensures that you don't lose any of the lovely oils that spray out of the skin.

Makes 12

MISO CARAMEL
175g double cream
2½ tbsp miso
175g caster sugar
75g water

WHITE CHOCOLATE MUDCAKE
150g unsalted butter
100g white chocolate chips, plus 75g finely chopped
120ml milk
¼ tsp vanilla extract
a pinch of sea salt
120g caster sugar
2 eggs
180g self-raising flour

MISO CARAMEL BUTTERCREAM
200g unsalted butter, softened
320g icing sugar, sifted

WHITE CHOCOLATE & SESAME DECORATIONS
100g white chocolate
1 tbsp black sesame seeds

BLACK GANACHE
100g dark chocolate chips (54% cocoa solids)
100g double cream
1 tbsp black cocoa powder

MISO CARAMEL CUPCAKES

Cupcakes

I can't remember the first time I came across miso caramel, but I remember it really appealed to my love of all things sweet and salty. In the same way that Marmite boosts the umami notes in our Sticky Toffee Cake (page 239), miso adds a curious savouriness to the caramel filling in these cupcakes, without tipping them into savouryland.

FOR THE MISO CARAMEL
Measure the cream into a jug and have it ready nearby, along with the miso.

In a medium saucepan, combine the sugar and the water, giving it a little bit of a stir to ensure that all the sugar is evenly soaked. Bring the mixture to a simmer over a low–medium heat and, without stirring at all (no matter how tempting), allow to bubble away for a few minutes until it begins to colour. Keep your eye on it and let it bubble away until it becomes a beautiful rich amber colour.

When the caramel has reached optimum amber, take it off the heat and add the cream, bit by bit, stirring quickly and carefully. Remember this is incredibly hot! Once all of the cream has been stirred in, add the miso and stir until completely dissolved.

Leave to cool completely, then pop it in the fridge.

FOR THE WHITE CHOCOLATE MUDCAKE
Preheat your oven to 190°C (170°C fan) and line a 12-hole cupcake tin with paper cases.

In a small saucepan over a low heat, melt together the butter, 100g of white chocolate, milk, vanilla and salt, stirring occasionally to make sure it doesn't catch and burn on the bottom of the pan. Leave to cool for 5 minutes or so.

In a large mixing bowl, whisk together the sugar and eggs until pale and a bit fluffy. Pour in the white chocolate mixture and whisk to combine. Add the flour and whisk until you have a smooth, lump-free batter, then add the remaining 75g finely chopped white chocolate and stir to combine.

Distribute the batter among the paper cases until they are three-quarters full, then bake for 18–20 minutes or until a toothpick inserted into the centre comes out clean Leave to cool.   >

< FOR THE MISO CARAMEL BUTTERCREAM

In a stand mixer fitted with the paddle attachment, or a large mixing bowl, beat the butter for at least 5 minutes on a high speed until it has turned almost white in colour and is nice and whippy. Add half of the sifted icing sugar and beat for 3-5 minutes, then repeat with the remaining icing sugar. You should have a very pale, almost white buttercream that is a bit too stiff. Add half of the miso caramel you made earlier and beat it in thoroughly. Make sure you taste it and add a bit more caramel if you want a stronger miso flavour.

FOR THE WHITE CHOCOLATE & SESAME DECORATIONS

Line a baking sheet with greaseproof paper or a silpat.

Melt the white chocolate as described on page 112, then pour it onto the prepared baking sheet and spread it out evenly using a palette knife or spatula until about 2mm thick. While it is still wet, sprinkle the black sesame seeds evenly over the top. If your chocolate is tempered, it will begin to set pretty quickly. If you haven't tempered it, that's okay, just pop it in the fridge for a bit to allow the chocolate to firm up. When it's almost set, use a round cookie cutter (3-4cm/1¼-1½in is a good diameter) to cut the discs, then leave to set completely before removing them.

TO FINISH

Remove the centres of your cupcakes using an apple corer (do not throw these away, they can be used as bribes for your children, or snacks for yourself!).

Put the remaining miso caramel into a piping bag and fill the cupcakes holes with it.

Pop the buttercream into a piping bag with a large round nozzle and pipe a generous blob on top of each cupcake. Pop them into the fridge for 10-15 minutes while you make the black ganache.

Make a dark chocolate ganache, as instructed on page 52, then sift in the black cocoa powder and stir it all to completely combine.

Remove the cupcakes from the fridge and, turning each one upside down, dip them into the black ganache until it reaches halfway up the sides of the icing. Leave to set for a couple of minutes before topping each cupcake with a sesame and white chocolate disc.

Makes 12

PREP
1 x batch of Blueberry
 Goo (page 60)

GRANOLA TOPPING
30g honey
10g soft light
 brown sugar
1 tbsp water
⅛ tsp vanilla extract
1 tbsp sunflower oil

50g rolled/porridge oats
15g pumpkin seeds,
 roughly chopped
15g sunflower seeds
10g sesame seeds
15g almonds, finely
 chopped
a pinch of sea salt
a pinch of ground
 cinnamon

YOGHURT SPONGE
155g self-raising flour

¼ tsp bicarbonate of soda
140g caster sugar
a pinch of sea salt
⅛ tsp ground nutmeg
85g olive oil
190g plain yoghurt
2 eggs
¼ tsp vanilla extract

**BLUEBERRY
AND YOGHURT
BUTTERCREAMS**
285g unsalted butter,
 softened

¼ tsp sea salt
450g icing sugar, sifted
1–2 tbsp Blueberry
 Goo (see Prep)
1–1½ tbsp plain yoghurt

**ADDITIONAL TOPPINGS
(OPTIONAL)**
banana chips, freeze-
 dried raspberry or
 strawberry pieces,
 coconut flakes –
 whatever you fancy,
 it's your breakfast!

BREAKFAST BOWL CUPCAKES

Cupcakes for breakfast? I wouldn't necessarily recommend chowing down on these for the most important meal of the day, but if you want to, I won't stop you! The sponge features olive oil and yoghurt, which might sound weird but makes it amazingly light and tangy. They're filled with blueberry goo and finished with a crunchy sweet granola. I've included enough granola to decorate your cupcakes with a bit left over for breakfast (if you're not eating the cupcakes for breakfast already, that is).

————

Make your Blueberry Goo as directed on page 60 and set aside until ready to use.

FOR THE GRANOLA TOPPING
Preheat your oven to 170°C (150°C fan) and line a baking tray with greaseproof paper.

In a small saucepan, melt the honey, sugar, water, vanilla and sunflower oil over a low heat, stirring occasionally until all of the sugar has dissolved.

In a medium bowl, whisk together the oats, seeds, almonds, salt and cinnamon. Pour over the honey mixture and stir to combine.

Spread the mixture over the baking sheet and bake for 20 minutes, then take it out to give it a stir. Reduce the oven to 150°C (130°C fan) and bake for a further 20 minutes until it's all golden.

Remove from the oven and leave to cool completely, then transfer it to an airtight container until you need it.

FOR THE YOGHURT SPONGE
Increase the oven to 190°C (170°C fan) and line a 12-hole cupcake tin with paper cases.

In a medium bowl, whisk together the flour, bicarb, sugar, salt and nutmeg.

In a separate bowl, whisk together the olive oil, yoghurt, eggs and vanilla until really well combined. Add the dry ingredients to the wet ingredients and stir with the whisk until you have a completely lump-free, smooth batter.

Distribute the batter evenly among the paper cases until they are three-quarters full. Bake for 18–20 minutes until the tops are golden and springy to the touch. Leave to cool.   >

95

< FOR THE TWO FLAVOURS OF BUTTERCREAM

In the bowl of your stand mixer fitted with the paddle attachment, or in a medium bowl, beat together the butter and salt for about 5 minutes on a high speed until the butter has lost its yellow colour and is pale and fluffy. Add the icing sugar in two stages, beating really well on a high speed for 3–5 minutes after each addition.

Remove roughly two-thirds of the mixture (or exactly, if you want to be like me, ha ha) to a separate bowl and add the blueberry goo. Beat well for a few minutes until light and fluffy. If you feel as if it needs a bit more goo, go ahead and add some.

Add the yoghurt to the remaining third of buttercream and beat well for a few minutes. Add more yoghurt if it feels too stiff.

Cover both buttercreams and set aside until you're ready to decorate.

TO FINISH

Remove the centre of each cupcake using your trusty apple corer.

Put the leftover blueberry goo into a piping bag and use it to fill the cupcake holes.

Fill two piping bags fitted with round nozzles with each of the flavours of buttercream. Pipe one fairly large blob of blueberry buttercream on top of each of the cupcakes, then follow that with a smaller blob of the yoghurt buttercream on top.

How you arrange the toppings is entirely up to you, but Sally insisted that ours should resemble one of those cute breakfast bowls you might get on holiday in Bali (or at home, if you are one of those types of people who really goes to town making their own breakfast!). Carefully arrange your granola, plus any other yummy bits and pieces you are using, such as banana chips or freeze-dried fruit, into neat rows on top of the yoghurt butterc ream blob, or even the entire cupcake, if that's your thing.

Makes 12

PREP
1 x batch of Cinnamon
Pie Crumb (page 64)
1 x batch of Salted
Caramel (page 42)

APPLE CRISPS
1 small apple, cored (Cox
or Braeburn work well)

APPLE SAUCE FILLING
300g apple (about 1
Bramley or 2 Braeburn),
peeled, cored and cut
into 1cm/½in chunks
50g unsalted butter
50g soft dark
brown sugar
1 tsp ground
cinnamon

SYRUP SPONGE
115g unsalted butter
115g soft light
brown sugar
225g golden syrup
1 egg
150g milk
225g self-raising
flour, sifted

**CINNAMON
BUTTERCREAM**
285g unsalted
butter, softened
¼ tsp sea salt
450g icing sugar,
sifted
½ tsp ground
cinnamon
1½ tbsp milk

APPLE PIE CUPCAKES

Can anyone tell we're obsessed with a good old-fashioned pud here at Crumbs & Doilies? I mean, what's not to love? Sweet, tart apple sauce, soft, syrupy sponge, spicy cinnamon buttercream and a sprinkling of Cinnamon Pie Crumb, topped off with drizzled caramel and an apple crisp. It's a bloomin' dreamboat of a cupcake!

———

Make the Cinnamon Pie Crumb (page 64) and Salted Caramel (page 42) and set aside.

FOR THE APPLE CRISPS

Preheat your oven to 120°C (100°C fan) and line a baking sheet with greaseproof paper.

Cut the apple in half and use a sharp knife or a mandoline to slice it very thinly. Aim for slices 1–2mm thick and watch your fingers! Cut them as uniformly as possible so that they all bake evenly. Place the apple slices on the baking sheet, making sure they don't overlap, then bake for 1½–2 hours, turning them over halfway through. If you remove them from the oven and they still feel a bit bendy after sitting on the counter for a few minutes, put them back into the oven for 10 minutes at a time until you have achieved perfect crispiness!

FOR THE APPLE SAUCE FILLING

Put all of the ingredients into a small pan and bring to a simmer over a medium heat. Cover with a lid and let it cook gently for around 10 minutes until the apples have completely softened, stirring occasionally. Leave to cool completely.

Once it's cooled, if the butter seems to have separated from the apple, just give it a good stir with a fork to bring it back together.

FOR THE SYRUP SPONGE

Preheat your oven to 190°C (170°C fan) and line a 12-hole cupcake tin with paper cases.

Melt together the butter, sugar and golden syrup in a medium saucepan over a low heat, stirring constantly until all of the sugar has dissolved. Leave to cool for 5 minutes.

In a mixing bowl, whisk the egg and milk until smooth, then gradually whisk in the cooled syrup mixture. Add the flour in two stages, whisking thoroughly after each addition until there are no lumps. Transfer the mixture to a jug for easy pouring.   >

Cupcakes

< Distribute the batter evenly among the paper cases until they are three-quarters full. Bake for 18–20 minutes until the cakes are springy to the touch and a skewer comes out clean when inserted into the middle. Leave to cool completely.

FOR THE CINNAMON BUTTERCREAM
In the bowl of a stand mixer, or a large mixing bowl, beat the butter and salt on a high speed for about 5 minutes until whippy and very pale in colour. Add half of the sifted icing sugar and the cinnamon, and beat for 3–5 minutes, then repeat with the remaining icing sugar until you have a fluffy but slightly stiff, and almost white buttercream. Add the milk a little at a time to achieve the right consistency, which should be smooth, spreadable and able to hold its shape, then beat for a further 3–5 minutes to finish.

TO FINISH
Using an apple corer, remove the centres of the cupcakes. Fill a piping bag with the apple sauce, then use this to fill the holes.

Fill a large piping bag fitted with a round nozzle with the buttercream, then pipe big, chubby blobs on top of each cupcake.

Finish with a drizzle of salted caramel, a cluster of cinnamon pie crumb and an apple crisp.

Makes 12

PREP
1 x batch of Salted
 Caramel (page 42)
100g Burnt Butter (page
 56), softened

BUTTERY PRETZEL BASE
90g salted pretzels,
 finely ground

25g unsalted
 butter, melted
20g golden syrup

BURNT BUTTER SPONGE
125g self-raising flour
100g caster sugar
25g soft light
 brown sugar
¼ tsp sea salt

¼ tsp bicarbonate
 of soda
100g Burnt Butter
 (see Prep)
25g unsalted butter,
 softened
2 eggs
1½ tbsp milk

**SALTED CARAMEL
BUTTERCREAM**
200g unsalted
 butter, softened
320g icing sugar, sifted
½ x batch of Salted
 Caramel (see Prep)

TO FINISH
extra salted pretzels

SALTED CARAMEL PRETZEL CUPCAKES

A true C&D classic, this is an unashamedly salty-sweet powerhouse of a cupcake that'll surely convert anyone who doesn't really get the whole salted caramel thing. Soft, fluffy sponge baked atop a buttery pretzel base and sitting beneath a delicious mound of sweet and salty caramel buttercream, topped off with more crunchy pretzels, this cupcake will have you drooling.

——

Make the Salted Caramel (page 42) and Burnt Butter (page 56) and set aside.

FOR THE BUTTERY PRETZEL BASE
Line a 12-hole cupcake tin with paper cases.

Mix the ground pretzels, butter and golden syrup in a bowl until the mixture resembles damp sand.

Spoon a tablespoon of the mixture into each of the paper cases and press down firmly using something small and flat, such as a shot glass or the end of a rolling pin. Set aside.

FOR THE BURNT BUTTER SPONGE
Preheat your oven to 190°C (170°C fan).

In the bowl of a stand mixer fitted with the paddle attachment, or a large mixing bowl, sift together the flour, both sugars, salt and bicarb. Add both of the butters, then the eggs, and beat together for about 30 seconds on a medium–high speed. Add the milk, then beat again for another 30 seconds or so, giving the bowl a good scrape down the sides and bottom halfway through to make sure you get every last bit. You should have a lovely smooth, light brown batter.

Distribute the batter evenly among the paper cases until they are three-quarters full. Bake for 18–20 minutes until the tops spring back when pressed. Leave to cool.

FOR THE SALTED CARAMEL BUTTERCREAM
In a stand mixer fitted with the paddle attachment, or a large mixing bowl, beat the butter on a high speed for at least 5 minutes until the butter has turned really pale in colour and is nice and whippy.   >

< Add half of the sifted icing sugar and beat for 3–5 minutes, then repeat with the remaining icing sugar. You should have a very pale, almost white, buttercream that is a bit too stiff. Add half of the salted caramel you made earlier to the buttercream and beat it thoroughly. Give it a taste and if you feel as though it needs a bit more salt, then go right ahead!

TO FINISH
Remove the centres of the cupcakes with an apple corer, being careful not to go all the way through the pretzel base. Add these to your nibble stash or store in your freezer to make cake pops with another day.

Pop the remaining half of the salted caramel into a piping bag and pipe it into the holes, making sure you don't overfill them.

Put the salted caramel buttercream into a large piping bag fitted with a round nozzle and pipe a generous blob on top of each cupcake.

To finish, sprinkle some crushed pretzels all around the edges of the cupcakes and crown the tops with one or two whole pretzels. If you have any leftover salted caramel, you could even top them with another drizzle – why the heck not?!

Makes 12

PREP
1 x batch of Blackberry
Goo (page 60)

APPLE SAUCE
300g apple (1 large
Bramley or 2 Braeburn),
peeled and cored
50g unsalted butter
50g soft light brown
sugar
1 tsp ground cinnamon

GRANOLA TOPPING
30g honey
10g soft brown sugar
1 tbsp water
⅛ tsp vanilla extract
1 tbsp sunflower oil
50g rolled/porridge oats
15g pumpkin seeds,
roughly chopped
15g sunflower seeds
10g sesame seeds
15g almonds, finely
chopped
a pinch of sea salt
a pinch of ground
cinnamon

APPLE SPONGE
140g apple, peeled
and cored (we like
Braeburn, Bramley or
Cox varieties)
125g self-raising flour
¼ tsp bicarbonate
of soda
100g caster sugar
25g soft light brown
sugar
125g unsalted butter,
softened
2 eggs
1 tsp treacle

**BLACKBERRY
BUTTERCREAM**
285g unsalted butter,
softened
a pinch of sea salt
450g icing sugar, sifted
1½ tbsp Blackberry Goo
(see Prep) or jam

TO FINISH
12 fresh blackberries

BLACKBERRY APPLE CRUMBLE CUPCAKES

Cupcakes

Towards the end of summer, we are blessed with an abundance of apples and blackberries here in the UK and, if you're lucky, you can easily forage both while walking about, even in the city. One of the best things to do with them is, of course, an apple and blackberry crumble. Filled with a tart apple sauce, topped with a beautifully and naturally pink blackberry buttercream and finished with crunchy granola to replicate the classic pud, this is one of our favourite seasonal cupcake flavours.

_____

Make the Blackberry Goo (page 60) in advance, so that it is cool for when you need to use it.

FOR THE APPLE SAUCE
Chop the apple into 1cm/½in cubes.

Combine all of the ingredients in a saucepan and bring to a simmer over a medium heat. Cover with a lid, reduce the temperature to low and allow it to bubble for about

10 minutes, giving it a stir every once in a while to help the apples heat evenly and break down a bit, until you have a nice thick sauce. Leave to cool.

FOR THE GRANOLA TOPPING
Preheat your oven to 170°C (150°C fan) and line a baking tray with greaseproof paper.

Melt together the honey, sugar, water, vanilla and oil in a small saucepan over a low-medium heat, stirring until all of the sugar has completely dissolved.

Meanwhile, combine all of the dry ingredients and spices in a mixing bowl and, when the sugar/honey solution is ready, pour it over the dry ingredients and stir thoroughly so everything is well coated.

Spread the mixture over the baking tray and bake for 20 minutes, then take it out and give everything a stir to break it up. Reduce the oven to 150°C (130°C fan) and bake for a further 20 minutes.   >

< Remove from the oven and leave to cool, then break up any big nuggets and put it all into an airtight container until you need it.

FOR THE APPLE SPONGE

Increase the oven to 190 °C (170 °C fan) and line a 12-hole cupcake tin with paper cases.

Coarsely grate the apple into a bowl. You then need to squeeze the juice out. The best way to do this is to use a potato ricer (like a giant garlic press), but if you don't have one, put all of the grated apple into a clean tea towel or muslin, twist the top and squeeze the juice into a bowl. Keep the bowl of juice to use later in the cupcake sponge.

Put 100g of the grated, strained apple into the bowl of a stand mixer fitted with the paddle attachment, or a mixing bowl. Sift in the flour, bicarb and sugars, then add the butter and eggs and mix on a medium speed for about 30 seconds to combine.

Add 1½ tablespoons of the reserved apple juice and the treacle and beat the mixture for another 30 seconds, giving it a stop 'n' scrape halfway through to catch any bits that got stuck to the bottom of the bowl.

Distribute the batter evenly among the paper cases until they are three-quarters full. Bake for 18–20 minutes until they are springy to the touch. Leave to cool.

FOR THE BLACKBERRY BUTTERCREAM

In a stand mixer or mixing bowl, beat the soft butter and salt on a high speed for at least 5 minutes until it is very pale and whippy. Add the sifted icing sugar in two stages, beating for 3–5 minutes after each addition. Add the blackberry goo (or jam) and beat it in until you have a beautiful pink, smooth, spreadable, voluptuous buttercream, adding more goo if you feel it's too stiff. Cover and set aside until you are ready to assemble.

TO FINISH

Use an apple corer to remove the centres of the cupcakes, then put the apple sauce into a piping bag and use it to fill the cupcake holes.

Put the buttercream into a piping bag fitted with a star nozzle and pipe generous bright pink swirls on top of each cupcake. Place a blackberry into the middle of the icing on each cupcake and surround that with the granola topping.

Makes 12

WHITE CHOCOLATE MUDCAKE
150g unsalted butter
100g white chocolate
120ml milk
¼ tsp vanilla extract
a pinch of sea salt
2 eggs
120g caster sugar
180g self-raising flour

BLACK SESAME SWISS MERINGUE BUTTERCREAM
1 x batch of Swiss Meringue Buttercream (page 40)
3-4 tbsp black sesame seeds, roasted for 5 minutes in the oven and cooled

CANDIED BLACK SESAME SEEDS
2 tbsp black sesame seeds, roasted for 5 minutes in the oven and cooled
2 tbsp water
2 tbsp icing sugar, sifted

WHIPPED WHITE CHOCOLATE FILLING
75g white chocolate chips
75g double cream

TO FINISH
50g white chocolate chips, melted

BLACK SESAME & WHITE CHOCOLATE CUPCAKES

If there's one cupcake flavour that customers are surprised by, it's this one. Those people to whom black sesame is unfamiliar sometimes need a little gentle persuasion, but this almost always results in delight! Black sesame has a unique roasty, toasty, nutty flavour unlike anything else and it partners brilliantly with the sweetness of white chocolate.

—

Preheat your oven to 190°C (170°C fan) and line a 12-hole cupcake tin with paper cases.

FOR THE WHITE CHOCOLATE MUDCAKE
In a small saucepan over a low heat, melt together the butter, white chocolate, milk, vanilla and salt, stirring occasionally to make sure it's well combined and doesn't get too hot and catch on the bottom of the pan. Leave to cool for 5 minutes or so.

In a large mixing bowl, whisk together the eggs and sugar until pale and a bit fluffy. Pour in the cooled white chocolate mixture and whisk to combine, then add the flour and whisk until you have a smooth, lump-free batter.

Distribute the batter evenly among the paper cases until three-quarters full. Bake for 18–20 minutes or until a toothpick inserted into the centre of a cake comes out clean. Leave to cool.

FOR THE BLACK SESAME SWISS MERINGUE BUTTERCREAM
Make the Swiss Meringue Buttercream as directed on page 40 and set aside.

Meanwhile, process the roasted sesame seeds in a food processor until they have transformed into a loose, smooth paste. This can take up to 20 minutes. If you don't have a food processor, you can smoosh the seeds into a stiff paste in a pestle and mortar, but your topping will look slightly different to ours. Stir the paste through the Swiss meringue buttercream until it's thoroughly combined. Cover and set aside until you are ready to decorate your cupcakes.   >

< FOR THE CANDIED BLACK SESAME SEEDS

In a small bowl, mix together the toasted black sesame seeds, water and icing sugar until the seeds are evenly coated.

Line a small baking tray with greaseproof paper, then spread the seed mixture over the tray. Bake at 190°C (170°C fan) for 10 minutes.

Leave to cool completely, then break into tiny nuggets and set aside.

FOR THE WHIPPED WHITE CHOCOLATE FILLING

In a medium bowl, melt together the white chocolate and double cream, either in the microwave in 30-second bursts, stirring well each time, or over a bain-marie. Stir the mixture to ensure it's all smooth and melty, then leave to cool to room temperature.

When cool, whip the mixture with an electric hand mixer until the yellowy colour has turned very pale and you have a silky, creamy mixture. It will still be quite runny – don't panic that it's not stiff! Pop the mixture into a piping bag.

TO FINISH

Remove the centres of the cupcakes using an apple corer. Keep your children, partners, flatmates or family members quiet with these little nuggets. Fill the holes with the whipped white chocolate filling.

Put the buttercream into a piping bag fitted with a large star nozzle and top each cupcake with a generous blob. Finish with a drizzle of melted white chocolate and a sprinkle of the candied sesame topping.

Makes 12

PREP
1 x batch of Strawberry Goo (page 60)
1 x batch of Plain Pie Crumb (page 64)
1 x batch of Swiss Meringue Buttercream (page 40) mixed with 2–3 tbsp Strawberry Goo

BUTTERY SHORTBREAD BASE
15g unsalted butter, melted
10g golden syrup
130g shortbread biscuits, crushed to a fine crumb

STRAWBERRY SPONGE
125g self-raising flour, sifted
¼ tsp bicarbonate of soda
125g caster sugar
125g unsalted butter, softened
2 eggs
2 tbsp Strawberry Goo (see Prep)

STRAWBERRY CREAM FILLING
100g double cream
2 tbsp Strawberry Goo (see Prep)

TO FINISH
200g white chocolate chips
½ tsp cocoa butter, melted
pink oil-based food colouring
freeze-dried strawberries, crushed (optional)

STRAWBERRY SHORTCAKE CUPCAKES

Cupcakes

Listen, I'm not gonna lie, these cupcakes take dedication and stamina. So much so, that we actually had to take them off our menu in the shop because they just take so long to make. They've got just about every conceivable element going: a buttery biscuit base, a filling, the sponge, the buttercream, the dip AND a pie crumb, because why the hell not?! But what they take away in hours they giveth back in downright deliciousness, and I guarantee you will forget how much effort they took when you're popping the third one into your mouth!

———

Make the Strawberry Goo (page 60), Plain Pie Crumb (page 64) and Swiss Meringue Buttercream (page 40), whisking in 2–3 tablespoons of Strawberry Goo at the end. Cover and set aside.

Preheat your oven to 190°C (170°C fan) and line a 12-hole cupcake tin with paper cases.

FOR THE BUTTERY SHORTBREAD BASE
In a bowl, mix all the ingredients thoroughly until the mixture resembles damp sand and will keep its shape when squeezed together. Scoop a tablespoon of the mixture into each of your paper cases and use the back of a spoon or a shot glass to press the crumbs down into a packed, even layer.

FOR THE STRAWBERRY SPONGE
In the bowl of a stand mixer fitted with the paddle attachment, or a mixing bowl, sift the flour, bicarb and sugar, then add the butter and eggs and beat for 30 seconds on a medium speed until thoroughly combined, stopping halfway to scrape down the sides and bottom of the bowl. Add the strawberry goo and beat for another 30 seconds until you have a smooth batter.

Distribute the batter evenly among the paper cases on top of the shortbread base until they are three-quarters full, then bake for 18–20 minutes until the tops spring back when pressed. Leave to cool.   >

< **FOR THE STRAWBERRY CREAM FILLING**

In a medium bowl, whip together the cream and the strawberry goo with a balloon whisk to 'floppy peak' consistency. Fill a piping bag with the mixture.

TO FINISH

Remove the centre of each cupcake using an apple corer and pipe the cream filling into the holes.

Put the buttercream into a large piping bag with a round nozzle, then pipe generous blobs on top of each cupcake. Place the cupcakes into the fridge to chill and set a little.

In a small heatproof bowl over a bain-marie, or in the microwave in short bursts, melt the white chocolate, then add the melted cocoa butter, which will help keep your chocolate shiny and soft. Add a couple of drops of the pink food colouring and mix well, then leave to cool for 5 minutes.

Carefully dunk the tops of the buttercream blobs into the pink chocolate, allowing the excess to dribble off before turning right side up. While the chocolate is still wet, finish with some crushed freeze-dried strawberries (if using) and a cluster of pie crumb nuggets. Leave to set before devouring. Or not, and get melted pink chocolate all over your face… Up to you!

Makes 12

PREP
1 x batch of Lime Curd
(page 58)
a tiny amount of green
food colouring
(optional)

LIME SPONGE
125g self-raising flour
¼ tsp bicarbonate
of soda
125g caster sugar
125g unsalted butter,
softened
2 eggs
zest of 2 limes
2 tbsp lime juice

HIBISCUS WATER
200ml water
25g dried hibiscus flowers

HIBISCUS BUTTERCREAM
285g unsalted butter,
softened
¼ tsp sea salt
450g icing sugar, sifted
1½ tbsp Hibiscus Water
(see above)

HIBISCUS GLAZE
235g icing sugar, sifted
a small pinch of sea salt
½ tbsp golden syrup
50ml Hibiscus Water
(see left)

TO FINISH
edible flowers

HIBISCUS & LIME CUPCAKES

Adding an infusion made with steeped, dried hibiscus flowers produces an intense and totally natural deep pink colour that I kind of just want to live in. Not only that, it has a really unique floral yet tangy flavour that pairs wonderfully with lime. And who ever said 'pink and green should never be seen' had clearly never seen, let alone eaten, one of these cupcakes!

Make the Lime Curd for the as directed on page 58 and set aside.

FOR THE LIME SPONGE
Preheat your oven to 190°C (170°C fan) and line a 12-hole cupcake tin with paper cases.

In the bowl of a stand mixer fitted with the paddle attachment, or a mixing bowl, sift together the flour, bicarb and sugar. Add the butter and eggs, then zest the limes over the top so you don't lose any valuable oils. Beat on a medium speed for 30 seconds or until the ingredients are well combined. Add the lime juice and beat for a further 30 seconds,stopping halfway to give the bowl a good scrape down the sides and bottom.

Distribute the batter evenly among the paper cases until they are three-quarters full. Bake for 18–20 minutes, or until the tops are lovely and golden and spring back when pressed. Leave to cool.

FOR THE HIBISCUS WATER
In a small pan, combine the water and dried hibiscus flowers. Bring to the boil over a medium heat, then reduce to a simmer and cook for a couple of minutes. Turn off the heat, cover and allow to steep until cool.

Strain out the flowers and set aside the ridiculously pink liquid until you need it.

FOR THE HIBISCUS BUTTERCREAM
In a stand mixer fitted with the paddle attachment, or a large mixing bowl, beat the butter and salt on a high speed for around 5 minutes until very pale. Add the icing sugar in two stages and beat for 3–5 minutes on a high speed after each addition. Add the hibiscus water a tablespoon at a time, beating well after each addition, adding as much as you need to get the buttercream to a smooth, whippy, spreadable consistency and a beautiful pink colour.

TO ASSEMBLE
Remove the centres of your cupcakes using an apple corer (saving the little nuggets for cake pops or a midway point reward).   >

<	If you are colouring your lime curd green, do this now using a very small amount of green food colouring paste. The green colour will look amazing with the pink of the hibiscus! Pop the curd into a piping bag and fill the cupcake holes one by one, making sure you don't over-fill them. Keep back any leftover curd and refrigerate to use on your morning toast or another cake!

Fill a big piping bag fitted with a large round nozzle with your lovely pink buttercream and pipe generous chubby blobs on top of each cupcake. Once they're all done, put them into the fridge to firm up a little bit for about 15 minutes. This will make dipping a lot easier.

FOR THE HIBISCUS GLAZE
While the cupcakes are chilling, make the glaze. In a small bowl, mix together the icing sugar, salt, golden syrup and hibiscus water until you have a smooth, very bright pink glaze. Cover the bowl with clingfilm so it doesn't form a crust while your cupcakes are chilling.

TO FINISH
Once the cupcakes are chilled, carefully turn each cupcake upside down one by one and dip into the little bowl of hibiscus glaze. Allow any excess to run off before turning them right side up and finishing them off with a couple of edible flowers for decoration.

Makes 12

PREP
1 x batch of Meringue
Poops (page 45)
(optional)

**ROASTED STRAWBERRY
PURÉE**
500g strawberries,
  hulled and halved
20g caster sugar

**STRAWBERRY RIPPLE
SPONGE**
125g self-raising flour

125g caster sugar
a pinch of sea salt
¼ tsp bicarbonate of soda
125g unsalted butter,
  softened
2 eggs
2–6 tbsp Roasted
  Strawberry Purée
  (see left)

YUZU BUTTERCREAM
285g unsalted butter,
  softened
¼ tsp sea salt
450g icing sugar, sifted
1½ tbsp yuzu juice

ROASTED STRAWBERRY & YUZU CUPCAKES

It had never occurred to me that you could roast a strawberry, but once I had tried it I was hooked, roasting them up by the punnet-load. Gently macerating the strawberries with a little sugar and then cooking them low and slow in the oven draws out the tart, intensely flavoured juice, transforming it into a syrup as it cooks and leaving the soft, sweet fruit ready to be used in so many ways, including in this cupcake! Yuzu, with its fragrant citrus flavour, is the perfect accompaniment. You can find 100% yuzu juice online and in some supermarkets.

Make the Meringue Poops as directed on page 45 and set aside.

FOR THE ROASTED STRAWBERRY PURÉE
Preheat your oven to 170°C (150°C fan).

Place the strawberries and sugar into a bowl and stir so that all the strawberries are covered in sugar and they begin to macerate. Spread them out on a deep baking tray and bake for 30 minutes, then leave to cool slightly.

Strain the strawberries, without stirring, through a sieve, saving the bright red,

syrupy juice. Set the syrup aside until ready to decorate.

Place the strained fruit into a small food processor or even the bowl of a pestle and mortar and pulverise until you have a smooth purée. Leave to cool.

FOR THE STRAWBERRY RIPPLE SPONGE
Increase the oven to 190°C (170°C fan) and line a 12-hole cupcake tin with paper cases.

In the bowl of a stand mixer fitted with the paddle attachment, or a medium mixing bowl, sift together the flour, sugar, salt and bicarb. Add the butter and eggs and beat together on a medium speed for around 30 seconds until well combined. Add 2 tablespoons of the strawberry purée, then beat for a further 30 seconds until well combined, stopping halfway to scrape the sides and bottom of the bowl.

Now we're going to ripple! Take a tablespoon of the strawberry purée and plop it into the bowl on top of the batter. Take a couple of dessert spoons and start scooping the mixture up, gathering the batter and some of the purée as you go, and popping it into the paper cases. Don't get too enthusiastic   >

< with the mixing here, as what we are trying to achieve is ripples and pockets of the strawberry through the sponge. Add more strawberry purée whenever you run out of ripple and keep going until you have filled all of your paper cases three-quarters full.

Bake for 18–20 minutes until the tops spring back when pressed. Leave to cool.

FOR THE YUZU BUTTERCREAM

In the bowl of a stand mixer fitted with the paddle attachment, or a mixing bowl, beat the butter and salt together for about 5 minutes until the yellow butter has turned a lovely pale creamy colour. Add the sifted icing sugar in two stages, beating for 3–5 minutes after each addition.

Add the yuzu juice bit by bit, to achieve a spreadable consistency that holds its shape, and beat again for 3–5 minutes, adding more juice if you want more flavour and you think the buttercream can take more liquid.

Cover and leave at room temperature until you start the assembly.

TO FINISH

Remove the centres of the cupcakes using an apple corer. Put the remaining strawberry purée into a piping bag and use it to fill the holes.

Pop the yuzu buttercream into a large piping bag fitted with a star-shaped nozzle and pipe generous swirls on top of each cupcake.

Drizzle a small amount of the intense strawberry syrup on top of each cupcake, allowing it to travel along the grooves of the icing. Top each one with a couple of little meringue poops to finish, if you like.

Makes 12

PREP
1 x batch of Milk
  Chocolate Swiss
  Meringue Buttercream
  (page 40)

PASSION FRUIT SPONGE
160g self-raising flour
¼ tsp bicarbonate of
  soda
130g caster sugar
a pinch of sea salt
50g passion fruit
  purée (see Tip)
140g plain yoghurt

2 eggs
85g sunflower oil
¼ tsp vanilla extract

PASSION FRUIT CURD
50g unsalted butter,
  cold and cubed
zest of ½ lemon
65g caster sugar

65g passion fruit purée
1 egg
3 egg yolks

CHOCOLATE AND
PASSION FRUIT DISCS
100g milk chocolate
1½ tbsp freeze-dried
  passion fruit chunks

MILK CHOCOLATE PASSION FRUIT CUPCAKES

We've got Dane to thank for this recipe, after he finally made us the passion fruit and milk chocolate macarons he'd been banging on about for years. We loved the flavour so much that I insisted he made a cupcake version for the book. These are a perfect balance of tangy and fragrant passion fruit with sweet and smooth milk chocolate, which you're gonna love!

———

Make the buttercream as directed on page 40. Cover and set aside.

FOR THE PASSION FRUIT SPONGE
Preheat your oven to 190°C (170°C fan) and line a 12-hole cupcake tin with paper cases.

In a medium bowl, whisk together the flour, bicarb, sugar and salt.

In a separate larger bowl, whisk together the passion fruit purée, yoghurt, eggs, oil and vanilla.

Add the dry ingredients to the wet and stir together with a whisk until you have a smooth, lump-free batter. It's quite runny so you might want to transfer it to a jug.

Distribute the batter evenly among the paper cases until they are three-quarters full. Bake for 18–20 minutes until the tops are lightly golden and springy when pressed. Leave to cool.

FOR THE PASSION FRUIT CURD
Get your butter ready and pop it back into the fridge to keep it cold.

Bring a small amount of water to the boil in a medium saucepan, then reduce to a simmer for your bain-marie.

In a heatproof bowl, whisk together the zest, sugar, passion fruit purée, egg and egg yolks, then set the bowl over the simmering water. Keep it over a medium heat and stir constantly with a whisk. After 8 minutes or so it will begin to thicken up. Keep stirring it over the heat for another couple of minutes to achieve a lovely dollopy consistency, then remove the bowl from the heat, grab the butter from the fridge and whisk it in until it's all melted.

Pass the curd through a sieve to get rid of any bits, then cover the bowl with clingfilm and allow to cool completely.   >

119

< FOR THE CHOCOLATE AND PASSION FRUIT DISCS

Line a baking sheet with greaseproof paper or a silpat.

Melt the chocolate as described on page 19. Pour the chocolate over the baking sheet and spread it into a thin layer about 2mm thick using a palette knife. Sprinkle the freeze-dried passion fruit chunks evenly over the top while the chocolate is still wet, then leave the chocolate until it is almost set but still tacky to the touch. If tempered, the chocolate will start to set quickly at room temperature, but if you can't be bothered with tempering you may need to put the chocolate in the fridge.

When the chocolate is almost set, use a round cutter to cut out 12 discs. Leave to set completely before removing the discs.

TO FINISH

Remove the centre of each cupcake using an apple corer. Put the passion fruit curd into a piping bag and fill the holes with it, reserving a little for decorating.

Pop the buttercream into a large piping bag fitted with a star-shaped nozzle and pipe generous swirls on top of each cupcake.

Take a teaspoon and warm it in a cup of hot water. Dry it, then use the back of the spoon to create a little dip in the top of the buttercream. Fill this with the remaining curd and top with a chocolate and passion fruit disc.

TEAM TIP

We like to use passion fruit purée, which you can source online. It usually comes in 500g bags, so it's a good idea to portion it into smaller amounts and freeze it. However, you can also use fresh, ripe passion fruit, just remove the seeds by straining them through a sieve. You will need approximately 8–10 ripe passion fruit for this recipe.

Cupcakes

Makes 12

PREP
1 x batch of Chocolate
Pie Crumb (page 64)
made with an added
½ tsp ground
cinnamon
200g Caramelised White
Chocolate (page 54)
130g Burnt Butter
(page 56), softened

BANANA CARAMEL
175g caster sugar
95g water
50g super-ripe banana,
mashed with a fork
175g double cream

BANANA SPONGE
125g unsalted butter
125g super-ripe banana,
mashed
140g self-raising flour
90g caster sugar
35g soft light brown
sugar
rounded ¼ tsp
bicarbonate of soda
a pinch of sea salt
2 eggs
1½ tbsp whole milk

**BURNT BUTTER
BUTTERCREAM**
130g Burnt Butter (see
Prep)
225g unsalted butter,
softened
a pinch of sea salt
450g icing sugar, sifted
¼ tsp vanilla extract
1½ tbsp whole milk

TO FINISH
½ tsp cocoa butter,
melted

BANANARAMA CUPCAKES

Cupcakes

Packed full of banana flavour and combined with two of our favourite ingredients, Caramelised White Chocolate and Burnt Butter, then adorned with Chocolate Cinnamon Pie Crumb. This cupcake is a great example of the magic that can happen when you mix and match different elements and additions to create a whole new flavour.

———

Make the Chocolate Cinnamon Pie Crumb (page 64), the Caramelised White Chocolate (page 54) and the Burnt Butter (page 56) and set aside.

FOR THE BANANA CARAMEL

In a medium saucepan, combine the sugar and water and give the mixture a little stir to ensure all of the sugar is evenly soaked. Bring to the boil over a low–medium heat and let it bubble away, without stirring, until the mixture has turned a rich amber colour.

When you're happy with the colour, remove the pan from the heat and carefully stir in the mashed banana using a long wooden spoon. It will bubble up and steam and will be incredibly hot, so take care. When all of the banana is mixed through, stir in the cream, a little at a time, until everything is thoroughly combined and you have lovely smooth caramel. Pour it into a bowl and allow to cool completely before putting it in the fridge.

FOR THE BANANA SPONGE

Preheat your oven to 190 °C (170 °C fan) and line a 12-hole cupcake tin with paper cases.

In the bowl of a stand mixer fitted with the paddle attachment, or a large mixing bowl, beat together the butter, banana, flour, sugars, bicarb, salt and eggs, starting on a low speed to combine the ingredients then increasing the speed to medium–high and beating for 30 seconds. Add the milk and beat for a further 30 seconds, stopping to scrape the bottom and sides of the bowl halfway through.

Distribute the batter evenly among the paper cases until they are three-quarters full, then bake for 18–20 minutes until the tops are lovely and springy. Leave to cool.   >

< FOR THE BURNT BUTTER BUTTERCREAM

In the bowl of a stand mixer fitted with the paddle attachment, or a large bowl, beat together both of the butters and the salt on a high speed for at least 5 minutes until very pale and fluffy. Add half of the sifted icing sugar and beat quickly for 3-5 minutes, then repeat with the remaining icing sugar. Give the sides and bottom of the bowl a good scrape, then beat in the vanilla and then the milk, a little at a time, to achieve the right consistency, which should be smooth, whippy, spreadable and able to hold its shape. Put your buttercream into a piping bag fitted with a round nozzle.

TO FINISH

Remove the centre of each cupcake using an apple corer.

Fill a small piping bag with the banana caramel and use it to fill the cupcakes. You may have some left over but this is no bad thing as it's delicious drizzled on pretty much any dessert or ice cream!

Pipe neat, generous, swirling blobs of the buttercream on top of each cupcake, then pop them into the fridge for 15 minutes to firm up and chill out.

Melt the caramelised white chocolate in a bowl over a bain-marie or in the microwave in short bursts, then stir in the melted cocoa butter. Coconut oil makes a good substitute if you don't have cocoa butter. Leave to cool slightly, then transfer to a small bowl.

Dip each chilled cupcake upside down into the caramelised white chocolate topping and allow the excess to dribble back into the bowl.

Finish by sticking the chocolate cinnamon crumb all around the edges of the cupcake, leaving the top naked so you get a lovely contrast in the colours. Leave to set, then devour!

Makes 12

PREP
1 x batch of Chocolate
  Cupcakes (page 32),
  still warm
3 tbsp Amarena cherry
  syrup (see Tip)

KIRSCH BUTTERCREAM
285g unsalted butter,
  softened
a pinch of sea salt
450g icing sugar, sifted
1½ tbsp kirsch liqueur
  or cherry syrup from a
  jar of Amarena cherries
  (see Tip)

CHERRY CREAM FILLING
6 Amarena cherries,
  chopped (see Tip)
1 tbsp icing sugar, sifted
100ml double cream
2 tbsp cherry syrup
  (optional)

TO FINISH
chocolate shavings
2 tbsp cherry syrup
50g dark chocolate,
  melted
12 fresh cherries,
  with stems, chilled
  in the fridge

BLACK FOREST CUPCAKES

Maybe the reason I loved this cake flavour so much growing up was because of the irresistible combination of cherries, chocolate and cream. Or maybe it was the booze-soaked sponges. Either way, Black Forest Gateau is an absolute classic, which deserved the Crumbs & Doilies treatment! Amarena cherries bring an ultra-cherry flavour to these delicious cupcakes.

——

Make the chocolate cupcakes as directed on page 32.

Once your cupcakes are out of the oven, warm up the cherry syrup in a small saucepan or in the microwave.

Let the sponges cool for 10 minutes, then use a cocktail stick or skewer to poke a few holes in the top of each one. While the cupcakes and the syrup are still warm, use a pastry brush to soak the tops of the cakes with the lovely syrup. The holes and the warmth will ensure maximum absorption! Leave to cool completely.

FOR THE KIRSCH BUTTERCREAM
In the bowl of a stand mixer fitted with the paddle attachment, or a large bowl, beat the butter and salt on a high speed for at least 5 minutes until the butter has lost much of its yellow colour and is pale and whippy. Add the icing sugar in two stages, beating for at least 3–5 minutes after each addition. You should have a very, very pale, fluffy but too-stiff buttercream at this point.

Add the kirsch or Amarena cherry syrup a little at a time to achieve a smooth, spreadable consistency that holds its shape, then beat for another few minutes until you have a light, fluffy consistency, adding more liquid if it feels too stiff. Set aside while you make the filling.

FOR THE CHERRY CREAM FILLING
Chop up the cherries really finely, almost to a paste.

In a medium bowl, whisk together the icing sugar and cream until it's a lovely thick-but-floppy consistency. Fold in the cherries, plus the syrup if you like, then spoon the mixture into a piping bag.

TO FINISH
Remove the centres of the cupcakes using an apple corer (save them for nibbling on), then fill the cupcake holes with the cherry cream filling.   >

< Pop the buttercream into a large piping bag with a star nozzle, then pipe generous swirls on top of each cupcake.

Put your chocolate shavings onto a small plate, then carefully dip the edges of the iced cupcakes into them so that you end up with a chocolate 'collar' all around the bottom of the icing, leaving the top of the swirl exposed.

Drizzle a little more of the cherry syrup on top, so that it dribbles down into the grooves of the swirled icing.

Put the melted chocolate into a very small bowl. Take your cherries from the fridge and dip them into the chocolate one by one, just enough so that the chocolate comes halfway up the sides. Let the excess dribble off. If you've kept your cherries in the fridge the chocolate should set immediately, meaning you can pop them straight on top of the cupcakes to finish them off.

———

TEAM TIP
Fabbri Amarena cherries are the best things to use in this recipe and you can usually get them at a good Italian deli. If you struggle to find them, Maraschino cherries will do (Luxardo ones are brilliant). In a pinch, tinned cherries will also work, just reduce the syrup a little bit in a pan, as it can be rather thin.

TRAYBAKES

TRAYBAKES

Along with our cupcakes, we are known far and wide for our amazing brownies and traybakes. Never content with being basic, we've spent years developing recipes that have enhanced the humble brownie and the more traditional traybakes. Our most famous bakes, like the Caramel Cornflake Brownie and Biscoff Rocky Road, are now emulated up and down the country and beyond, much to our delight. In the case of the Caramel Cornflake Brownie, we literally can't open the shop without having them on the counter!

Aside from being versatile and delicious, good traybakes are usually quick and undaunting to make and have the added benefit of travelling well (in most cases!), making them perfect for parties and picnics. They can also be cut into generous slabs or little bite-sized pieces, meaning you can make them go as far as you need to. All of the following recipes make a 20cm/8in square bake, which can be cut into 9–16 pieces, or if you just want to take a fork to it, we won't judge you – we've all been there!

In this chapter you'll find everything from simple but satisfying 5-ingredient treats, to epic layered bakes that will wow the crowd! For tips on how to cut them up and get perfect, clean squares, check out the QR code to see how we do it.

Lining a brownie tin   Cutting a brownie

CARAMEL CORNFLAKE BROWNIE   132

CEREAL FUN BAR   134

BISCOFF ROCKY ROAD   136

TRIPLE DECKER BROWNIE   138

COOKIE CHEESECAKE   140

BANANA BLONDIE   142

MARATHON BROWNIE   144

CARAMEL APPLE CHEESECAKE   146

OG CORNFLAKE CRUNCH   148

RASPBERRY WHITE
CHOCOLATE BLONDIE   150

COOKIE DOUGH BROWNIE   152

LEMON MERINGUE BAR   154

S'MORES BROWNIE   157

STRAWBERRY SHORTCAKE
CHEESECAKE   160

BONFIRE BAR   163

CORNFLAKE CARAMEL
300g double cream
1¼ tsp vanilla extract
¾ tsp sea salt

450g caster sugar
150g unsalted butter,
cubed
190g plain cornflakes

CARAMEL CORNFLAKE BROWNIE

Our iconic Caramel Cornflake Brownie has been imitated the world over! And if a bake is going to take over the world it ought to be this one. Combining chewy cornflake caramel with the irresistibly fudgy C&D Chocolate Brownie, it's an utterly mouth-watering, totally addictive bite, which flies off the counter in the shop almost as soon as we've sliced it up!

———

Prepare the C&D Chocolate Brownie as directed on page 34 and leave to cool in the tin before refrigerating.

FOR THE CORNFLAKE CARAMEL
Mix the cream, vanilla and salt together in a small jug and set aside.

In a large saucepan, make a dry caramel by heating the sugar over a low heat. As the sugar begins to melt, stir it a little with a wooden spoon or heatproof spatula to ensure it caramelises evenly.

Once the sugar has all dissolved and turned a rich amber colour, remove from the heat and slowly pour in the cream mixture, a little at a time, stirring quickly. Once all of the cream is in and you have a smooth caramel, add the butter and stir to combine (if you have any nuggets of undissolved caramel, don't panic, just put the pan back over a low heat and stir to dissolve).

Put the pan back over a medium heat and fix a sugar thermometer to the inside. Heat the caramel, stirring occasionally, until it has reached 116°C.

Remove from the heat, then add the cornflakes, mixing thoroughly and carefully to coat every single flake.

TO FINISH
Remove the cooled brownie from the fridge and dump the still hot cornflake caramel mixture on top. Push it down and into all the corners of the tin using a wooden spoon, then leave to cool completely before putting into the fridge to set.

Once set, cut the brownie into squares and serve at room temperature.

———

TEAM TIP
Use a hot, clean knife each time you make a cut, to ensure you get nice clean slices!

Traybakes

**Makes 9 big or
16 small portions**

120g Rice Krispies
180g any fun colourful
    cereal (we've used
    Lucky Charms, Fruit
    Loops and Dunkaroos),
    plus extra to decorate

120g unsalted butter
300g white
    marshmallows
    (we like the little ones)
½ tsp sea salt

300g white chocolate
    chips
oil-based food colours
    in 2-3 shades

CEREAL FUN BAR

Of all the recipes we developed for this book, none have made us quite so weak at the knees as this six-ingredient delight! We all tried to resist it, but there is something about the sweet saltiness of the cereals and the nuttiness of the burnt butter that had us nibbling at it incessantly without even realising! Reminiscent of a classic childhood treat, but pimped, make this with your kids, make it for yourself, it doesn't matter why – just make it!

———

Grease and line a 20cm/8in square tin with greaseproof paper.

In a large bowl, combine the different cereals and give them a stir.

In a large saucepan, heat the butter over a medium heat to melt it. We like to use burnt butter in our cereal bars to add a lovely depth of flavour. To do this just keep it on the heat, stirring occasionally, until you begin to see little dark flecks appearing on the bottom of the saucepan and the smell transforms to a lovely warm nutty aroma.

Remove from the heat and, while the butter is still piping hot, add the marshmallows and salt and stir with a wooden spoon until all of the marshmallows have completely melted and combined with the butter to form a goopy, white, floppy mass.

Tip the marshmallow mixture onto the cereal and quickly and carefully stir it all together, making sure all of the cereal is coated in the mixture, then tip it all out into the prepared tin. Press it down with a spatula to create a compact, even layer and leave to cool completely.

In a microwave, or over a bain-marie, melt the white chocolate. Pour roughly three-quarters of it over the top of the cooled cereal mixture, then divide the remaining chocolate among separate bowls and colour it using oil-based food colourings (use just a small amount of each colour).

Transfer each coloured chocolate to small piping bags, one for each colour, and pipe a few lines of each over the top of the white chocolate layer. Alternatively you can use teaspoons to drizzle it. Use a cocktail stick or skewer to wiggle a marbled pattern through the coloured lines. Don't over-wiggle as this can cause the colours to combine too much and create a murky tone, which is NOT what you want on a Cereal Fun Bar! If you like, you can sprinkle some extra cereal on top for some more pizzazz. Leave to set either at room temperature or in the fridge, then remove from the tin and cut into super-fun pieces!

**Makes 9 big or
16 small portions**

500g white chocolate
300g Biscoff spread
50g unsalted butter
300g Biscoff cookies

¼ tsp sea salt
¼ tsp vanilla extract
200g mini marshmallows

BISCOFF ROCKY ROAD

An OG Crumbs & Doilies classic, which has been on the menu since we first opened and is showing no signs of waning in popularity. Everyone wants a piece of it! It's simple, a great bake to make with kids and we guarantee you'll be addicted!

——

Grease and line the base and sides of a 20cm/8in square tin with greaseproof paper.

Melt together the white chocolate, Biscoff spread and butter in a heatproof bowl using the microwave or a bain-marie.

While they're melting, break up the Biscoff cookies into little pieces.

Next, mix the salt and vanilla into the melted Biscoff mixture, along with all but a handful of the mini marshmallows and most of the broken-up Biscoff cookies. Stir together, making sure everything is evenly coated.

Spoon the whole lot into your prepared tin and even out a little with the back of a spoon. Obviously, it's pretty lumpy, so don't get too precious, just make sure it reaches all the corners and edges.

Decorate the top with the marshmallows and biscuit pieces you held back, then chill in the fridge for around 1 hour until completely set.

Carefully, remove from the tin and cut into squares using a large knife.

——

TEAM TIP
Leave the greaseproof paper on the sides of the tin a little long so that you can use it to lift out the Rocky Road once it's set.

Makes 9 big or
16 small portions

PREP
1 x C&D Chocolate
Brownie (page 34)

RICE KRISPIE BASE
35g unsalted butter
a pinch of sea salt
90g mini white
 marshmallows
70g Rice Krispies

NOUGAT
35g unsalted butter
135g caster sugar
40g evaporated milk
140g Marshmallow Fluff
¼ tsp vanilla extract

**MILK CHOCOLATE
GANACHE**
200g milk chocolate
 chips
100g double cream

TRIPLE DECKER BROWNIE

One of my favourite chocolate bars growing up, the Double Decker was just asking to be added to our list of 'bakified' desserts and treats. It's a masterclass in chewiness! We took the crispy, light base, the soft, chewy nougat and sandwiched our dense and fudgy chocolate brownie in between for the ulimate chew-fest, then topped the whole lot off with sweet milk chocolate ganache!

––––

Prepare the C&D Chocolate Brownie as directed on page 34 and leave to cool in the tin.

FOR THE RICE KRISPIE BASE
In a medium saucepan, heat the butter over a low-medium heat, stirring constantly, until it begins to bubble and little flecks of brown start to appear on the bottom of the pan. Remove from the heat and add the salt and marshmallows, stirring carefully and allowing the residual heat from the butter to melt the marshmallows. Add the Rice Krispies and stir them through, then immediately empty the mixture on top of the chocolate brownie and press it down all over so you have an even layer that has reached all the corners of the tin. Leave to cool, then transfer to the fridge to set for 15–20 minutes.

When set, carefully remove the entire brownie from the tin and remove the paper. Re-line the empty tin, then turn the whole brownie upside down so that the Rice Krispie layer is on the bottom, then carefully return it back to the tin.

FOR THE NOUGAT
In a saucepan over a low-medium heat, melt the butter completely, then add the sugar and evaporated milk and heat, stirring constantly, until every grain of sugar has dissolved (or until 120°C on a sugar thermometer). This is really important if you want to have a chewy, rather than oozy, nougat.

Remove from the heat and, while the mixture is still hot, add the Marshmallow Fluff and vanilla and give it a good stir until thoroughly combined.

Pour the mixture on top of the brownie layer in the tin and spread evenly with a palette knife, then leave to cool.

FOR THE GANACHE
Make the ganache as directed on page 52, then pour it all over the top of the nougat layer and level out with a palette knife. Leave to cool and set in the fridge for 30 minutes before cutting into squares.

––––

TEAM TIP
We use our hands (wearing latex gloves, of course) to press the Rice Krispies onto the brownie layer – it's so much quicker!

Traybakes

138

Makes 9 big or
16 small portions

COOKIE TOPPING
75g unsalted butter,
  softened
115g soft light
  brown sugar
55g caster sugar
1 egg plus 1 egg yolk
½ tsp vanilla extract
145g plain flour
½ tsp sea salt
120g dark chocolate
  chips (54% cocoa
  solids), roughly
  chopped

BUTTERY BISCUIT BASE
225g Hobnobs, crushed
  to a fine crumb
70g unsalted butter,
  melted
10g golden syrup

CHEESECAKE FILLING
430g cream cheese
85g caster sugar
1 egg plus 1 egg yolk
¼ tsp vanilla extract

TO DECORATE
20g dark chocolate,
  melted
mini coloured chocolate
  buttons

COOKIE CHEESECAKE

This super bake was created by Rosie and Nikki, who - in a moment of madness - sandwiched cheesecake between two layers of cookie and baked it to create this marvel. Finished with a drizzle of chocolate and colourful chocolate buttons, it's a really fun dessert, perfect for a party!

———

Grease and line two 20cm/8in square loose-bottomed cake tins with greaseproof paper.

FOR THE COOKIE TOPPING
In a large bowl, beat all of the ingredients together, except for the chocolate chips, until well combined, then add the chocolate chips and stir through until evenly distributed.

Spread the dough evenly over the bottom of one of the tins and place in the fridge for 30 minutes until firm enough to handle.

FOR THE BUTTERY BISCUIT BASE
Preheat your oven to 190°C (170°C fan).

Stir all of the base ingredients together in a bowl until the texture is similar to damp sand and it holds together when you squeeze some between your fingers. Press the mixture firmly into the base of the other tin in an even layer.

Bake the base for 10 minutes, then remove and leave to cool completely.

FOR THE CHEESECAKE FILLING
Put all the ingredients into a stand mixer fitted with the balloon whisk, or a large bowl, and whip together on a medium-high speed for 5-7 minutes until pale and thick. Spread this mixture onto the biscuit base in an even layer using a palette knife.

Take the cookie dough slab from the fridge and remove it from the tin, keeping the greaseproof paper stuck to the bottom. Turn it upside down and place it into the tin, directly on top of the cheesecake layer, being careful not to press down too much, then peel away the paper.

Bake for 30–35 minutes until the cookie has turned a golden colour and there is a firm jiggle to it. Leave to cool before placing in the fridge to chill right down.

TO FINISH
Pour the melted chocolate into a small piping bag and drizzle zigzags all over the cooled cookie cheesecake. While the chocolate is still wet, sprinkle the coloured chocolate buttons on top to finish it off.

Makes 9 big or
16 small portions

PREP
120g Burnt Butter
 (page 56), melted

TO FINISH
240g soft light brown
 sugar (split into 40g
 and 200g)
40g unsalted butter
210g very ripe banana,
 chopped

3 eggs
1 tsp vanilla extract
215g plain flour, sifted
1 tsp sea salt
¼ tsp baking powder
160g pecans, toasted
 and roughly chopped

50g dark chocolate
 chunks
150g milk chocolate
 chunks

BANANA BLONDIE

Another brilliant recipe from Dane's archives, he created this back when everyone was going on and on about banana bread over lockdown. Always one to go the extra mile, Dane created this delectable alternative to what became the nation's favourite bake and we think it's even better than banana bread, thanks to the burnt butter, the generous amount of chocolate chips and the fudgy, slighty chewy texture.

———

Make the Burnt Butter as directed on page 56. Set aside.

Preheat your oven to 180°C (160°C fan) and grease and line a 20cm/8in square tin with greaseproof paper.

In a small saucepan over a medium heat, combine the 40g of sugar and the regular butter and heat until the butter has melted. Add the banana and cook for 8–10 minutes, stirring occasionally, until the banana has broken down quite a bit, the colour is deep and golden, and you have a few flecks of dark brown. Leave to cool.

In a medium bowl, combine the burnt butter with the remaining 200g of sugar and whisk together for a minute or so, just to combine. Whisk in the eggs and vanilla until thoroughly combined, then stir in the banana mixture. Sift in the flour, salt and baking powder, and stir until smooth. Finally, add most of the pecans and chocolate chunks, holding some back for decorating the top. Fold these through gently until evenly distributed.

Pour the batter into your prepared tin and sprinkle the reserved pecans and chocolate chunks on top, then bake for 30 minutes until a skewer inserted into the centre comes out a bit fudgy.

Leave to cool completely, then transfer to the fridge to set and reach peak fudginess before cutting into pieces.

Traybakes

Makes 9 big or
16 small portions

PREP
1 x C&D Chocolate
Brownie (page 34)

CHEWY CARAMEL
130g double cream
¾ tsp vanilla extract
¼ tsp sea salt
200g caster sugar
65g unsalted butter,
cold and cubed

NOUGAT
35g unsalted butter
135g caster sugar
40g evaporated milk
140g Marshmallow Fluff
¼ tsp vanilla extract
45g peanut butter
100g salted peanuts,
roughly chopped

GANACHE
150g dark chocolate
chips (54% cocoa
solids)
150g double cream

MARATHON BROWNIE

We used to freak out when, after sitting on the counter in the shop, the caramel and nougat in this bake would start to ooze out, so slowly it was imperceptible to the naked eye. But the more they oozed, the more customers wanted them! Choc-full of salty peanuts and rich chocolate, this bake has a little bit of everything. And as for the oozy fillings? We doubt this will last long enough for you to witness their bid for freedom!

———

Prepare the C&D Chocolate Brownie as directed on page 34. Leave to cool in the tin.

FOR THE CHEWY CARAMEL
Stir together the cream, vanilla and salt in a jug and set aside.

Heat the sugar in a saucepan over a low-medium heat. When it begins to melt and bubble at the edges, bring those melted bits into the middle of the pan with a wooden spoon or heatproof spatula, to ensure the sugar caramelises evenly. Stir occasionally until the sugar has completely dissolved and the caramel is a rich amber colour.

Remove from the heat and pour in the cream mixture, a little at a time, stirring quickly and carefully, then add the butter and stir it through the caramel as it melts.

Return the pan to a medium heat and cook until it hits 116°C on a sugar thermometer. Too low and the caramel won't set at all; too high and it will become impossibly chewy!

Once ready, pour the caramel immediately (and carefully) over the top of the cooled chocolate brownie, levelling with a palette knife if necessary. Leave to cool and set completely before beginning your nougat.

FOR THE NOUGAT
In a saucepan over a low–medium heat, melt the butter, then add the sugar and evaporated milk and heat, stirring constantly, until every grain of sugar has dissolved (and it has reached 120°C on a sugar thermometer). Remove from the heat and, while still hot, stir in the Marshmallow Fluff, vanilla, peanut butter and chopped peanuts until well combined.

Pop the nougat on top of the set caramel, spread evenly, then leave to cool.

FOR THE GANACHE
Make the ganache as directed on page 52, then pour it immediately all over the nougat to completely cover it. Pop it into the fridge to set for 1 hour before cutting into squares.

Makes 9 big or 16 small portions

PREP
½ x batch of Salted Caramel (page 42)

BASE
180g plain flour
65g soft light brown sugar
180g unsalted butter
a pinch of sea salt

CHEESECAKE FILLING
430g cream cheese
85g caster sugar
a pinch of sea salt
90g lightly whisked eggs (about 1½ eggs)
½ tsp vanilla extract

FOR THE APPLES
450g apples (about 1½ Bramley apples), peeled, cored and chopped into 1cm/½in cubes
3 tbsp caster sugar
3 tsp ground cinnamon
¼ tsp ground nutmeg

CRUMBLE TOPPING
135g soft light brown sugar
135g unsalted butter, cold and cubed
90g plain flour
a pinch of sea salt
60g rolled/porridge oats

CARAMEL APPLE CHEESECAKE

A melt-in-the-mouth baked cheesecake, crowned with an intensely fruity, cinnamon apple layer and topped off with a sweet and crunchy, crumbly topping, this is one of our favourites and makes a brilliant dessert to share among friends. Drizzle it with caramel to give it the full C&D treatment.

Make the Salted Caramel as directed on page 42 and set aside.

FOR THE BASE
Preheat your oven to 190°C (170°C fan) and grease and line a deep 20cm/8in square tin with greaseproof paper.

Combine all the base ingredients in a food processor and pulse until the mixture is just about to clump together. Tip it all out onto the work surface and knead briefly before pressing it into the lined tin in an even layer.

Bake for 20 minutes, then leave to cool.

FOR THE CHEESECAKE FILLING
In the bowl of a stand mixer fitted with the balloon whisk, or a large mixing bowl, whisk all the filling ingredients for around 5 minutes until thick and spreadable. If it's too thin, the apples will sink to the bottom. Pour it onto the baked crust and level out with a palette knife.

FOR THE APPLES
Toss the apples with the sugar and spices until evenly coated, then distribute evenly over the top of the cheesecake layer.

FOR THE CRUMBLE TOPPING
In a food processor, pulse all the ingredients except the oats until they begin to come together. If you aren't using a food processor, you can do this either by rubbing between your fingers and thumbs, or using a pastry cutter. Add the oats and stir through.

Sprinkle the mixture over the top of the apples, then bake for 45 minutes until the apples are soft and the crumble is lovely and golden.

Remove from the oven and leave to cool completely before popping into the fridge to set.

To serve, drizzle with some salted caramel.

Makes 9 big or 16 small portions

PREP
½ x batch of Malty Cornflakes (page 68)

CORNFLAKE BISCUIT BASE
225g Hobnobs, or similar biscuits, crushed to a fine crumb
45g Malty Cornflakes (see Prep)

50g unsalted butter, melted
10g golden syrup

CORNFLAKE CARAMEL
300g double cream
1¼ tsp vanilla extract
¾ tsp sea salt

450g caster sugar
150g unsalted butter, cubed
190g plain cornflakes

GANACHE
200g milk chocolate
100g cream

OG CORNFLAKE CRUNCH

A Nikki original and the birthplace of Malty Cornflakes (page 68) and the Caramel Cornflake Brownie (page 132), this is one of those bakes that you look at and think, 'I couldn't possibly finish a whole piece of that', but realise later that you've eaten the entire thing without noticing! It's chewy and crunchy, and yet another example of why salty and sweet should meet in a treat.

───

Make the Malty Cornflakes as directed on page 68 and set aside.

FOR THE CORNFLAKE BISCUIT BASE
Preheat your oven to 190°C (170°C fan) and grease and line the base and sides of a high-sided 20cm/8in square tin.

In a mixing bowl, combine all of the ingredients with a wooden spoon until the mixture resembles damp sand and holds its shape if you squeeze some between your fingers. Tip it into the prepared tin and press into the base to form a compact, even layer. Bake for 10 minutes, then leave to cool.

FOR THE CORNFLAKE CARAMEL
Combine the cream, vanilla and salt in a jug and set aside.

In a large saucepan, heat the sugar over a medium heat until the edges of the sugar begin to melt and colour. Start to move the sugar around a bit with a wooden spoon to ensure it caramelises evenly. When all the sugar has dissolved and the liquid is a rich amber colour, remove from the heat and add the cream mixture, a little at a time, stirring quickly and carefully until fully incorporated. Add the butter and stir through until melted and combined.

Return the pan to a medium heat and pop a sugar thermometer into the pan. Heat the mixture to 116°C, then remove from the heat and stir in the cornflakes thoroughly.

Tip the cornflake caramel into the tin on top of the base and, using a spatula or the back of a wooden spoon, press it into the base and corners in a compact layer. Leave to cool.

TO FINISH
Make the ganache as directed on page 52, then immediately pour it over the top of the caramel cornflake layer. Tip the tin around or spread with a palette knife to cover the top completely. Sprinkle over a few handfuls of malty cornflakes. Allow to set before slicing.

Traybakes

Makes 9 big or
16 small portions

PREP
150g Caramelised White
  Chocolate (page 54),
  cut into chunks

½ batch of Raspberry
  Goo (page 60)
135g Burnt Butter
  (page 56), melted and
  cooled a bit

TO FINISH
335g soft light
  brown sugar
3 eggs
1¼ tsp vanilla extract
270g plain flour
¼ tsp baking powder

¼ tsp sea salt
10g freeze-dried
  raspberries (optional)
150g white
  chocolate chips

RASPBERRY WHITE CHOCOLATE BLONDIE

Just like with brownies, the trick to great blondies is making them fudgy and ever so slightly chewy, rather then cakey. These blondies deliver that in spades and are so full of juicy, tart raspberry goo and caramelised white chocolate that you'll find them difficult to resist.

———

Make the Caramelised White Chocolate and Raspberry Goo as directed on pages 54 and 60, and set aside. Make the Burnt Butter according to the instructions on page 56 and leave to cool but not set. Or, if you have some already made, melt it back to liquid form.

Preheat your oven to 190°C (170°C fan). Grease and line the bottom and sides of a 20cm/8in square baking tin.

In a large bowl, add the sugar to the burnt butter and whisk to combine. You're not trying to add any volume here, so don't go crazy! Add the eggs and vanilla and whisk until well combined, then add the flour, baking powder and salt, and fold into the mixture to create a lovely batter with no lumps.

Add the freeze-dried raspberries, if using, almost all the chocolate chips and the caramelised chocolate chunks to the batter. Keep some back to scatter onto the top for decoration. Stir through until evenly distributed.

Empty the batter into your prepared tin, levelling it out with a palette knife or spatula, then push the remaining chocolate chips into the top of the batter.

Put your raspberry goo into a piping bag and inject it into the blondie batter, pushing the tip of the bag, or nozzle if you're using one, right into the bottom of the batter and pulling up while squeezing, so that you end up with 15-20 pools of goo going from the bottom to the top all over the blondie.

Bake for 30-35 minutes until a skewer inserted into the centre comes out a little bit fudgy. Cook for longer if you'd rather have a more cakey blondie.

Leave to cool completely before putting in the fridge for at least a couple of hours. Chilling it will result in the ultimate fudgy blondie!

Traybakes

COOKIE DOUGH
200g plain flour
140g caster sugar
90g soft light brown
  sugar
1 tsp sea salt

240g unsalted butter,
  softened
1 tsp vanilla extract
4 tbsp plain yoghurt
100g dark chocolate
  chips

CHOCOLATE GANACHE
150g dark chocolate
  chips (54% cocoa
  solids is nice here)
150g double cream

COOKIE DOUGH BROWNIE

We used to have a customer in the shop who would get quite emotional when we had this on the menu and almost inconsolable when it wasn't. It's no wonder this is a fan favourite, with its rich chocolate ganache, pleasingly soft, choc-chip-studded cookie dough and our chewy chocolate brownie. It's a real finger-licking delight!

––––––

Prepare the C&D Chocolate Brownie as directed on page 34 and leave to cool in the tin.

FOR THE COOKIE DOUGH
Preheat your oven to 190°C (170°C fan).

Spread the flour evenly over a baking sheet and bake for 10 minutes, stirring halfway. This will ensure there is no nasty bacteria lurking in the raw flour. Leave to cool completely.

When the flour is cool, combine all the cookie dough ingredients, except the chocolate chips, in a bowl and beat together thoroughly until light in colour (with an electric hand mixer this should take about 30 seconds). Gently mix in the chocolate chips.

Spread the mixture over the top of the cooled brownie in its tin and level it with a palette knife, then put into the fridge to chill and set for 30 minutes.

FOR THE CHOCOLATE GANACHE
Make the ganache according to the instructions on page 52, then pour it immediately over the cookie dough layer. Even out with a palette knife or the back of a spoon.

Pop the tin into the fridge and allow to chill completely before cutting into squares.

Traybakes

**Makes 9 big or
16 small portions**

SHORTBREAD BASE
150g unsalted butter,
 softened
85g caster sugar
¾ tsp sea salt
225g plain flour

LEMON CURD FILLINGS
200g plus 50g cold
 unsalted butter,
 chopped
zest of 3 lemons
195g lemon juice
195g caster sugar
3 eggs plus 9 egg yolks

TOPPING
1 x batch of Italian
 Meringue (page 48)

LEMON MERINGUE BAR

Traybakes

This recipe, which we made especially for the book, was born out of a desire for a punchier, lemon-meringue-pie bar. We knew that we wanted the base to be chunkier than pastry but still short, so shortbread was the obvious choice, but whenever we tried it with baked lemon custard, the shortbread became soggy no matter what we did. Then, Dane came up with the genius suggestion of a whipped lemon curd and hey presto!, the Lemon Meringue Bar was born. Chunkier than a pie and lemonier than an actual lemon!

_____

FOR THE SHORTBREAD BASE
Preheat your oven to 170°C (150°C fan) and grease and line a 20cm/8in square, loose-bottomed cake tin with greaseproof paper.

In the bowl of a stand mixer fitted with the paddle attachment, or a large mixing bowl, stir or slowly beat together the butter and sugar. You don't want to make it pale and fluffy, you just want to combine the two well.

Add the salt and flour and stir together gently until the mixture starts to clump together in little nuggets. At this point, get your hands into the bowl to squeeze the nuggets together a bit before

emptying the whole lot into the prepared tin. Use the back of a spoon or your hands to press the dough into an even layer on the bottom of the tin.

Bake for 30 minutes until the top of the shortbread is a light golden colour. Remove and leave to cool completely.

FOR THE LEMON CURD FILLINGS
First, chop the butter into 1cm/½in cubes and divide between two bowls: 200g and 50g respectively. Put these into the fridge to keep cold. Also, to get prepared, grab two medium bowls to use later.

Bring a small amount of water to the boil in a medium saucepan, then reduce to a simmer over a medium heat. This is for your bain-marie.

In a heatproof bowl, whisk together the lemon zest, juice, sugar and lastly the eggs and egg yolks, then set on top of the simmering pan. Heat for 8–10 minutes, stirring constantly with the whisk, until it becomes lovely and thick. Remove from the heat.

Working quickly, put one-third of the curd into one of your reserved bowls and   >

< two-thirds into the other (extra points for weighing it and doing it perfectly!). To the smaller amount of curd, add the 50g of cold butter and whisk in until it's melted. Likewise, add the 200g of cold butter into the larger amount of curd and whisk in. Sieve both curds while they're still warm to get rid of any bits, then cover with clingfilm and leave to cool before putting into the fridge to chill completely, at least 2 hours.

TO FINISH

Take the larger bowl of curd from the fridge and whisk it for 5–10 minutes until pale in colour and light and whippy. Spread this out all over the shortbread base with a palette knife.

When the whipped curd layer has chilled and set a bit, put the remaining lemon curd into a piping bag and pipe it all over the bottom curd layer. Use a palette knife to even it out to a flat layer.

Put it into the fridge to chill while you make the Italian Meringue (page 48).

Fill a large piping bag with the Italian Meringue and cut a large hole in the tip. Pipe it all over the lemon curd layer, then spread out with the palette knife. Doing it in this way will prevent the layers beneath from being displaced by aggressive spreading before it's had a chance to set. Of course, if you like the piped look on top, lean into that and forget your palette knife! Use a kitchen blowtorch to lightly toast the meringue or put the whole tin under a very hot grill for a few seconds to achieve perfect toastiness.

Remove from the tin and slice with a hot, clean knife (a blowtorch comes in handy here too!).

**Makes 9 big or
16 small portions**

BUTTERY BISCUIT BASE
60g unsalted butter,
  melted
200g digestive biscuits
  or Graham Crackers,
  crushed to a fine,
  even crumb

30g golden syrup (you
  can use corn syrup or
  honey, if you like)

BROWNIE
165g unsalted butter
165g dark chocolate
3 eggs
330g caster sugar
135g plain flour

45g cocoa powder
½ tsp sea salt
½ tsp baking powder

GANACHE
30g dark chocolate
  chips
30g double cream

TO FINISH
1 x batch of Italian
  Meringue (page 48)
a handful of digestive
  biscuits, broken into
  pieces

S'MORES BROWNIE

There isn't a single baked good that
we haven't 'S'moresed' at C&D. We have
a s'mores cupcake, s'mores cake (see
page 230), cookie cup and, of course,
brownie, which is our favourite way to
s'more! Eating it is like biting through
a slightly caramelised, toasted cloud into
an extremely chocolatey, chewy dream,
with extra s'mores vibes provided by the
buttery biscuit base. This bake is the best
reason to buy yourself a kitchen blowtorch.

———

Preheat your oven to 190°C (170°C fan)
and grease and line a high-sided 20cm/
8in square, loose-bottomed tin.

FOR THE BUTTERY BISCUIT BASE
In a bowl, mix together the butter, biscuit
crumbs and syrup until the mixture
resembles damp sand.

Empty the mixture into the prepared tin and
press down using the back of a spoon or the
underside of a glass until you have a tightly
packed, even layer that reaches all of the
corners and edges. Set aside.

FOR THE BROWNIE
In a bain-marie set over a medium heat, or
in the microwave in 30-second bursts, melt
the butter and chocolate together, stirring
occasionally to combine. Leave to cool
a little.

In a separate bowl, whisk together the
eggs and sugar until they have doubled
in volume and turned quite pale. Add
the cooled chocolate and butter and fold
in slowly. Sift in the remaining brownie
ingredients, folding them in carefully to
make a thick, smooth batter.

Pour the batter into the tin on top of
the biscuit base, levelling the mixture
with a spoon or a palette knife, if necessary.
Bake for 28–30 minutes until just set and
an inserted skewer comes out a bit gooey.
If you prefer your brownie a bit more cakey,
pop it back in for 1–2 minutes.

Leave to cool completely in the tin, then
put into the fridge to chill.   >

< TO ASSEMBLE

Make your Italian Meringue as directed on page 48, then plonk the whole lot on top of the chilled brownie and spread it into an even layer using a palette knife. As you will be torching it, you want to create a bit of drama on the top, so use the back of a spoon, a palette knife or even a skewer to create swirls.

Make sure you have cleared your work surface of tea towels, love letters and anything else that might catch fire, then blowtorch the top of the meringue, being careful not to set light to the greaseproof paper, until you have a lovely brown and white swirly pattern and can smell the unmistakable aroma of burnt sugar (alternatively, place it under a hot grill for a few seconds).

Make the ganache according to the instructions on page 52, then drizzle it over the top of the meringue in a random, haphazard way, finishing the whole thing off by poking the broken bits of biscuit into the Italian Meringue so that they are jagged and upright.

———

TEAM TIP

For really sharp, clean edges to your brownie squares, if you still have your blowtorch handy, give your clean knife a quick flame every time you make a cut. It will take a bit longer but it's worth it if you want pretty, perfectly square pieces.

Makes 9 big or
16 small portions

PREP
1 x batch of Plain Pie
Crumb (page 64)
1 x batch of French
Meringues (page 45),
broken into pieces

ROASTED STRAWBERRIES
500g strawberries, washed,
hulled and halved
30g caster sugar

SHORTBREAD BASE
150g unsalted butter,
softened
85g caster sugar

¾ tsp sea salt
225g plain flour

STRAWBERRY CHEESECAKE
600g cream cheese
100g icing sugar, sifted
3–4 tbsp syrup from the
roasted strawberries
180g double cream

**PINK CHOCOLATE
DRIZZLE**
30g white chocolate
chips
pink oil-based food
colouring

STRAWBERRY SHORTCAKE CHEESECAKE

Traybakes

A while ago, Sam asked the team to make him a cake with strawberry shortcake vibes. We came through with the Strawberry Shortcake Cupcakes (page 110) and he loved them! So when we began brainstorming ideas for the book, we knew we had to take the flavour to the next level. With the help of my new favourite ingredient, roasted strawberries, this cheesecake delivers a punchy strawberry hit, and at the same time is creamy, crunchy and, of course, delicious.

—

Make the Plain Pie Crumb as directed on page 64 and the French Meringues as directed on page 45 and set aside.

FOR THE ROASTED STRAWBERRIES

Preheat your oven to 170°C (150°C fan).

In a bowl, toss the strawberries together with the sugar until they are coated and beginning to get all juicy. Spread them out all over a baking tray so that they are all separate, then bake for 30 minutes.

Remove from the oven and strain the strawberries through a sieve set over a bowl

to separate the fruit from the super-charged syrup. Allow to cool completely.

FOR THE SHORTBREAD BASE

Grease and line a 20cm/8in square baking tin with greaseproof paper.

In the bowl of a stand mixer, or a medium mixing bowl, beat together the butter, sugar and salt, just to combine. Add the flour and mix through slowly until the mixture resembles breadcrumbs.

Tip the mixture out onto the work surface and bring it together with your hands, squeezing the crumbs together until you have a clumpy, crumb-like dough (but don't overwork it, otherwise you will lose that 'shortness').

Tip the crumbly nuggets into the tin and press down so that so that you have an even layer of dough covering the bottom. Bake for 30 minutes until it's a lovely golden colour, then leave to cool completely in the tin. ＞

< FOR THE STRAWBERRY CHEESECAKE

Put half of the roasted strawberries into a blender or food processor and blitz until smooth. Spread the mixture over the shortbread base in an even layer.

In a medium bowl, whip together the cream cheese, icing sugar and strawberry syrup with a whisk or an electric hand mixer until well combined and smooth.

In a separate bowl, whip the cream with a whisk or electric hand mixer until it's at the 'floppy' stage, then add it to the cream cheese mixture and whip everything together until the mixture is fluffy, smooth and a little stiffer and spreadable.

Chop the remaining roasted strawberries into small pieces, then add them to the cheesecake mixture and stir through until they are well distributed.

To avoid displacing the strawberry purée layer, it's best to put the cheesecake mixture into a large piping bag with a big hole in the end, to pipe it on top of the base. Use an offset palette knife or the back of a spoon to spread the mixture out so that it covers the base in a nice even layer. Pop it into the fridge for 20 minutes.

TO FINISH

Melt the white chocolate in either a bain-marie or gently in the microwave, then add a tiny amount of food colouring (if using) and mix thoroughly. Transfer to a small piping bag.

Remove the cheesecake from the fridge and wiggle the pink chocolate over the top in zigzags or spirals, or however you fancy. Decorate with nuggets of pie crumb and broken-up meringues. Return it to the fridge for 3–4 hours or ideally overnight to set completely, before carefully removing it from the tin and slicing with a warmed knife to get those clean edges!

———

TEAM TIP

Use a piece of greaseproof paper to squash down the shortbread dough in the tin to achieve a nice level top.

**Makes 9 big or
16 small portions**

Ginger Honeycomb
100g golden syrup
200g caster sugar
1 tsp bicarbonate
of soda
½ tsp ground ginger

NUTTY GINGER BASE
170g ginger biscuits,
crushed to a fine crumb
80g unsweetened
desiccated coconut
60g lightly toasted
pecans, finely chopped
110g unsalted butter
45g caster sugar
a pinch of sea salt
¼ tsp vanilla extract
30g cocoa powder
1 egg

SMOKY CARAMEL
1 heaped tsp lapsang
souchong tea
150g double cream
¾ tsp vanilla extract
a pinch of sea salt
200g caster sugar
65g unsalted butter,
cold and cubed

GINGER CHEESECAKE
600g cream cheese
100g icing sugar, sifted

a pinch of sea salt
180g double cream
80g stem ginger,
finely chopped

GANACHE
150g dark chocolate
chips (54% cocoa
solids)
150g double cream
a pinch of smoked
sea salt

BONFIRE BAR

We created this recipe especially for the book. We wanted something that evoked a blustery autumnal evening, with bonfires and fireworks! Lapsang souchong tea gives the caramel a deep smokiness, while the filling and honeycomb topping are spiced with ginger to warm you up from the inside.

———

FOR THE GINGER HONEYCOMB
Grease and line a 20cm/8in baking tin or baking dish with greaseproof paper.

Heat the golden syrup and sugar in a medium saucepan with a sugar thermometer attached over a medium–low heat. Stir the mixture occasionally with a wooden spoon. It will start out stiff and solid but, as the syrup warms up and the sugar starts to dissolve, it will liquefy. Keep on the heat, bubbling away until the sugar is completely dissolved, the colour is beginning to deepen and the temperature reads 150°C.

Remove from the heat and add the bicarb and ginger, through a sieve, directly on top of the caramel. Stir quickly and thoroughly to distribute it through the caramel. The mixture will bubble up a lot, so take care.

When you have mixed it well, pour the bubbling caramel into the prepared tin. Don't be tempted to spread it out or interfere with it, otherwise you will lose the bubbles. Leave to cool and set completely.

Store the honeycomb in an airtight container until ready to use to prevent it from becoming sticky.

FOR THE NUTTY GINGER BASE
Grease and line the base and sides of a 20cm/8in square tin with greaseproof paper.

In a large bowl, mix together the ginger biscuit crumbs, coconut and pecans and set aside.

In a small saucepan, melt the butter. Remove from the heat and stir in the sugar, salt, vanilla and cocoa to form a smooth, dark mixture. Add the egg, then return to a medium heat and whisk together for a couple of minutes until you have a smooth, silky mixture.

Pour the wet mixture into the dry ingredients and mix until very well combined. Tip this out into the tin and press down with   >

< the back of a spoon until you have a compact, even layer. Place in the fridge for at least 30 minutes or until set firm.

FOR THE SMOKY CARAMEL

To infuse the cream, scatter the loose tea over the cream in a small saucepan and stir. Set it over a medium heat and cook until just beginning to steam. Remove from the heat and allow to steep for 5-10 minutes, then strain out the tea through a fine sieve.

Measure 130g of the infused cream into a small jug, then add the vanilla and salt and stir well to combine. Set aside.

In a medium saucepan with a sugar thermometer attached, heat the sugar over a medium-low heat. As the sugar begins to melt and bubble, use a wooden spoon to gently bring the melted sugar into the middle of the pan to encourage it to caramelise evenly. Allow the sugar to bubble away gently, stirring occasionally, until it has completely dissolved and is a lovely rich amber colour.

Remove from the heat and slowly pour the infused cream into the caramel a little at a time, stirring quickly and carefully. Keep stirring until well combined. Add the butter and stir through until melted, then return the pan to the heat until the temperature reaches 116°C.

Remove from the heat, allow the bubbles to subside a little, then pour it all over the nutty ginger base, tipping the tin to ensure that every corner is reached. Leave to cool before placing in the fridge to set.

FOR THE GINGER CHEESECAKE

In a medium bowl, whisk together the cream cheese, icing sugar and salt to a smooth, whippy consistency.

In a separate bowl, whip the cream until it's nice and floppy, then add it to the cheesecake mixture and whisk together until thick and spreadable. Add the finely chopped stem ginger and stir through until evenly distributed.

Tip this on top of the chilled caramel layer and spread out with a palette knife or spatula until the top is completely level. Chill in the fridge for 30 minutes.

TO FINISH

Make the chocolate ganache as directed on page 52, then pour it immediately over the top of the chilled cheesecake and spread out with a palette knife. Chill in the fridge for 3-4 hours, ideally overnight, to set.

Before serving, break the honeycomb into small chunks and stab the chunks into the ganache to create a jagged landscape of crunchy deliciousness that resembles a bonfire! Lastly, give the top a light sprinkling of smoked sea salt, then slice up and serve.

———

TEAM TIP

Putting the honeycomb onto the top just before serving will ensure it doesn't go sticky and bendy in the fridge.

COOKIES

COOKIES

We have always loved cookies and various ones have graced the counter since we opened, from Chewy Choc Chip Cookies and PB&J Sarnies to our famous Cookie Cups. It was during a fateful trip to New York that Sam, Sally and I first encountered the chunky, gooey cookies that were blazing a trail in NYC, like so many iconic bakes before them. Once we had tried these giant hunks of cookies, we decided that London deserved them too! So, Sally and Dane set about unpicking, experimenting, analysing and tweaking until at last we had our own version we could be proud of. Fast forward, and we now make more of our NY-style cookies than any other bake, sending boxes of them all over the country to satisfy the sweet-tooths of the nation!

Cookies are a great place to start with baking. They are usually pretty straightforward to make and lots of cookies can be frozen in their raw dough form so that you can just pop a couple in the oven when you fancy a nibble on something sweet. They are also great for sharing and can be made quickly (especially if you have a batch of frozen cookie dough balls in waiting). What's more, you don't need any special decorating skills to make them.

Here are a couple of QR codes, which will give you the scoop on how to get your cookies just right.

Balling an NY Cookie

Getting perfectly round cookies

WALNUT CHOC CHIP NY COOKIES 170

VELVET VOLCANO COOKIE CUPS 172

DOUBLE CHOC NY COOKIES 174

CHEWY CHOC CHIP COOKIES 176

PB&J SARNIES 178

RED VELVET NY COOKIES 180

GINGER CREAMS 182

BIRTHDAY CAKE NY COOKIES 184

SKILLET COOKIE 186

GINGER & BISCOFF NY COOKIES 188

COOKIE DOUGH COOKIES 190

APPLE CRUMBLE NY COOKIES 192

VEGAN BISCOFF SANDWICH COOKIES 194

CARAMEL PRETZEL COOKIE SARNIES 196

MALLOW WHEELS 199

TWICKS BITES 202

BISCOFF COOKIE CUPS 205

Makes 12 huge cookies

100g walnuts
230g unsalted butter,
    fridge-cold and cubed

160g caster sugar
160g soft light brown
    sugar
400g milk chocolate chips

200g self-raising flour
300g plain flour
¼ tsp sea salt
¼ tsp bicarbonate of soda

2 tsp baking powder
2 eggs

WALNUT CHOC CHIP NY COOKIES

In 2019, Sally, Sam and I went to NYC to eat our way around some of the best bakeries in the city. Unfortunately, a slipped disc meant I had to spend much of the trip lying down while the guys toured the city without me! It wasn't all bad though... on our return, Sally was determined to recreate the chunky, oozy cookies that ruled the streets of New York. She and Dane set to work developing our own versions, starting with this one. It was an instant classic: warm, gooey cookie perfection.

————

STAGE 1: BALLING
Preheat your oven to 190°C (170°C fan).

Roast the walnuts in the oven for 5 minutes, then remove and pour onto a clean tea towel. Gather the corners to enclose the nuts, then rub the cloth between your hands to remove the skins, which you can discard. Break or chop the walnuts up a bit and set aside.

In the bowl of a stand mixer fitted with the paddle attachment, or a mixing bowl, break up the cold butter on a medium speed for a few seconds. Add the sugars and mix for 30–45 seconds until nuggets begin to form, then add the chocolate chips and walnuts and mix a little to just combine. Add the flours, salt, bicarb and baking powder and stir through until the mixture looks sandy with some visible chunks of butter.

Whisk the eggs lightly, then pour them into the bowl with the rest of the ingredients. Mix for a few more seconds until big nuggets of dough begin to form and the sides of the bowl are clean. The key is not to overmix your dough. Chunky dough = chunky cookies.

Tip the dough onto your work surface and use digital scales to measure out 125g amounts. Gently squeeze the dough into balls, rather than rolling them (check out the QR code on page 168 to see it done!).

Put the balls into an airtight container and freeze for a minimum of 2 hours, ideally overnight.

STAGE 2: BAKING
Preheat your oven to 210°C (190°C fan) and line a baking sheet with greaseproof paper.

Remove the number of cookie balls you'd like to bake from the freezer (maybe you just want one as a treat, no judgement!) and put them onto the baking sheet, spaced out well, as they spread. Bake for 16 minutes until the outer shell is a little golden but the centres are still gooey.

Remove from the oven to cool. Optimum cooling time is 20 minutes to enjoy them at their gooey-centred, melty, oozy best.

Cookies

Makes about 22

PREP
½ x batch of Oreo
  Buttercream (page 36)
¼ x batch of Salted
  Caramel (page 42)
  in a piping bag
½ x batch of Cookie
  Dough (page 66),
  cut into tiny chunks

RED VELVET COOKIE CUPS
55g unsalted butter,
  softened
95g soft brown sugar
½ large egg (see Tip on
  page 206)
½ tsp vanilla extract
⅛ tsp red food colouring
  paste (not liquid)
115g plain flour
10g cocoa powder

¼ tsp sea salt
¼ tsp bicarbonate
  of soda

CHEESECAKE FILLING
145g cream cheese
30 caster sugar
½ large egg (see Tip
  on page 206)
¼ tsp vanilla extract

CHOCOLATE
GANACHE DRIZZLE
30g double cream
30g dark chocolate
  chips (70% cocoa
  solids)

VELVET VOLCANO COOKIE CUPS

Velvet Volcano was the first 'frankencake' flavour we created at C&D. An explosion of all the best bits and bobs we are often left with at the end of a day's baking, these cookie cups combine a red velvet cookie cup, vanilla cheesecake, cookie dough, Oreo buttercream, chocolate ganache and salted caramel, and we know you'll 'lava' them as much as we do.

———

Make the Oreo Buttercream (page 36), Salted Caramel (page 42) and Cookie Dough (page 66), cover and set aside.

FOR THE RED VELVET COOKIE CUPS
Lightly grease a 24-hole mini cupcake tin.

In the bowl of a stand mixer fitted with the paddle attachment, or a medium bowl, cream the butter and sugar together for 30 seconds, just to combine. Add the egg, vanilla and red food colouring, and beat until well combined. Sift in the flour, cocoa, salt and bicarb and fold it through to bring the dough together.

Use digital scales to weigh out 15g nuggets of the chilled dough and roll them into little balls (wear gloves as there can be a bit of colour transfer). Pop one into each of the holes of the tins. Using a flat-bottomed implement about 2.5cm/1in thick, such as a mini rolling pin, press down on top of each ball, allowing the dough to travel up the sides of the tin to the top. Pop the tin in the fridge while you make the cheesecake filling.

FOR THE CHEESECAKE FILLING
Preheat your oven to 190°C (170°C fan).

Put all the filling ingredients into a stand mixer fitted with a balloon whisk, or a medium bowl, and whisk for 5 minutes or so until thick and forming soft peaks. Transfer to a piping bag and fill each cookie cup with the mixture.

Bake for 10 minutes, then remove from the oven and leave to cool for 15–20 minutes. Prise them carefully from the tin and allow to cool completely. Taking them out too soon can cause the rims to break off.

FOR THE CHOCOLATE GANACHE DRIZZLE
Make the ganache as directed on page 52 and put it into a piping bag.

TO FINISH
Pipe a chubby blob of buttercream on top of each cookie cup, then drizzle with zigzags of the chocolate ganache and salted caramel. Top with chunks of cookie dough to finish.

Cookies

Makes 12

230g unsalted butter, fridge-cold and cubed

160g soft light brown sugar
160g caster sugar
400g dark chocolate chips

300g plain flour
130g self-raising flour
70g black cocoa powder (regular will be fine, just not as dark)

1 tsp sea salt
2 tsp baking powder
2 eggs plus 1 egg yolk

DOUBLE CHOC NY COOKIES

What do you do when the classic NY Choc Chip Cookie just isn't chocolatey enough? It's time to go Double Chocolate! You can make these without the black cocoa powder of course, but I urge you to scour the shelves and rev up your search engines because regular cocoa just won't deliver the same intense flavour as the black stuff, and also, they won't look quite as cool.

———

STAGE 1: BALLING

Beat the cold chunks of butter on a medium speed in a stand mixer fitted with the paddle attachment, or by hand in a mixing bowl, to break them up. Add the sugars and mix for 30–45 seconds until you start to see nuggets forming. Next, add the chocolate chips and mix briefly, then add the flours, cocoa, salt and baking powder and stir until the mixture is sandy with chunks of butter.

Whisk your eggs and yolk briefly in a separate bowl, then pour them into the mixture and stir until you end up with big chunky nuggets. Be careful not to overmix it.

Tip the dough onto a clean work surface and measure out 125g amounts, gently squeezing each into a ball. Resist the urge to roll them.

Put the balls into an airtight container and freeze for at least 2 hours, ideally overnight.

STAGE 2: BAKING

Preheat your oven to 210°C (190°C fan). Line a baking sheet with greaseproof paper.

Remove the number of cookie balls you'd like to bake from the freezer and put them onto the baking sheet, spaced out well, as they will spread. Bake for 16 minutes until the outside of each cookie is a black craggy shell and the inside is still soft and gooey.

Remove from the oven and leave to cool for at least 20 minutes, lest you burn your fingers and tongue on molten chocolate.

Makes 18

185g Burnt Butter (page 56), melted and cooled
215g soft light brown sugar

1 egg plus 1 egg yolk
2 tsp vanilla extract
225g plain flour
¾ tsp bicarbonate of soda

1 tsp sea salt
200g milk chocolate, chopped into chunks
200g dark chocolate, chopped into chunks
1 tsp flaked sea salt

CHEWY CHOC CHIP COOKIES

Have you spent a lifetime searching for the perfect chewy chocolate chip cookie? Then I'm happy to tell you the search is officially over! These cookies are irresistibly crisp, chewy and delicious thanks to the burnt butter, a frankly ridiculous ratio of choc chips to cookie and a sprinkling of flaky sea salt.

—

Preheat your oven to 190°C (170°C fan) and line a baking tray with greaseproof paper.

Put the cooled burnt butter into a large mixing bowl with the sugar and combine with a whisk. Add the egg, egg yolk and vanilla, and whisk until just combined. You're not trying to add air here. Add the flour, bicarb and salt, then use a spatula to stir together. Add most of the chocolate chips, keeping back a few for decorating, and stir them through the dough. It's rather a soft dough, so pop it into the fridge for about 30 minutes to make it easier to handle.

Weigh out 50g nuggets of the cookie dough and roll them into balls, studding the tops with a couple of the reserved chocolate chips (if you want to keep some of the dough back to bake another time, roll into balls and freeze them, adding a couple of extra minutes to the baking time when baking from frozen).

Bake in batches, placing the balls about 10cm/4in apart on the tray, for 7-9 minutes until the edges are browning ever so slightly but the centres of the cookies are still soft.

Remove from the oven, sprinkle with the flaked sea salt and leave to cool slightly before devouring them while still warm!

—

TEAM TIP
Nikki's neat trick for ending up with cookies that are perfectly round is to grab a large round cutter (bigger than the cookies) and, as soon as they've baked, place the cutter over each cookie and wiggle it around on the baking tray to nudge them into being perfect circles. To see this in action, check out the QR code on page 168.

Makes 10

120g unsalted butter, softened
100g soft light brown sugar
100g caster sugar
100g smooth peanut butter (we love Skippy)
1 egg
190g plain flour
1½ tsp baking powder
a pinch of sea salt

FILLING
150g smooth peanut butter
150g raspberry or grape jam

PB&J SARNIES

The combination of peanut butter and jam (or jelly) is a match made in school lunchbox heaven. In fact, I have the pairing on my toast every day. These little mini sandwiches have been one of my all-time favourite things on our menu since we opened and I get very excited when I see them on the counter. They're cute AND delicious!

———

In the bowl of a stand mixer fitted with the paddle attachment, or a large mixing bowl, beat together the butter, sugars and peanut butter until smooth and a little paler in colour. Add the egg and beat in thoroughly, then sift in the flour, baking powder and salt, folding it through the mixture until thoroughly combined.

Lay out a large piece of greaseproof paper, about 50cm/20in long, on your work surface. Spoon the soft dough into a rough sausage, about 30cm/12in long. The aim here is to fashion the dough into a kind of square sausage (a little bit like a mini loaf of bread!). Use the greaseproof paper to smooth the sides and top to tease it into shape. You can use something flat and sturdy, like a chopping board, to get the sides as straight as possible. Don't obsess over it though, because these don't stay super square after baking.

Once you're happy, wrap the dough with the greaseproof paper and place in the freezer for at least 1 hour.

Preheat your oven to 190°C (170°C fan) and line two baking sheets with greaseproof paper.

Remove the chilled dough from the freezer and use a sharp knife to cut it into slices that are 1cm/½in thick. Place them on the baking sheets at least 5cm/2in apart. Place any unused dough back in the freezer.

Bake for 10-12 minutes until the tops are golden. Leave to cool completely.

TO FINISH
Pair up cookies of a similar shape and size. On the TOP of one cookie, pipe little blobs of peanut butter and little blobs of jam all over the top, then cover with another cookie, topside-down, to complete the sandwich. Why, you ask? The bottoms of these cookies have a kind of toasty look, which works really well to make them look more like actual sandwiches! Keep going until you have a delicious pile of little PB&J sandwiches.

Cookies

179

Makes 12

230g unsalted butter, fridge-cold and cubed
160g soft light brown sugar
160g caster sugar
400g white chocolate chips
475g plain flour
12g cocoa powder
12g black cocoa powder (you can use all regular cocoa if you can't find black cocoa)
1 tsp sea salt
2 tsp baking powder
2 eggs
1 tsp vanilla extract
1 tsp red food colouring paste

RED VELVET NY COOKIES

Once our NY cookies began to take off, the question on everyone's lips was 'can you do a red velvet cookie?' Of course we can! Unmistakable with its red colour, this cookie version of the classic cake is chocolatey and vanilla-y in all the right places and packed full of white chocolate chips to give you a satisfying oozy cookie-break.

STAGE 1: BALLING

Beat the cold butter on a medium speed in a stand mixer fitted with the paddle attachment, or by hand in a mixing bowl, to break it up a bit. Add the sugars and mix for 30–45 seconds until you start to see nuggets forming. Next, add the chocolate chips and mix briefly, then add the flour, cocoa powders, salt and baking powder and stir until the mixture is sandy with a few small chunks of butter.

Whisk your eggs together with the vanilla and red food colouring in a separate bowl, then pour it all into the mixture and stir until you end up with a chunky, nuggety dough. Be careful not to overmix it.

Tip the dough onto a clean work surface and measure out 125g amounts, gently squeezing each into a ball. Resist the urge to roll them.

Put the balls into an airtight container and freeze for at least 2 hours, ideally overnight.

STAGE TWO: BAKING

Preheat your oven to 210°C (190°C fan). Line a baking sheet with greaseproof paper.

Remove the number of cookie balls you'd like to bake from the freezer and put them onto the baking sheet, spacing them out to allow for spreading. Bake for 16 minutes until the outer shell of each cookie is craggy and crisp and the insides are still a little wobbly.

Remove from the oven and cool for at least 20 minutes before eating.

TEAM TIP

Don't use regular liquid food colouring. It is nowhere near as concentrated as pastes or gels, so you'd need to use a lot to achieve a rich red colour and that would alter the consistency of the dough and ultimately ruin your cookies.

Cookies

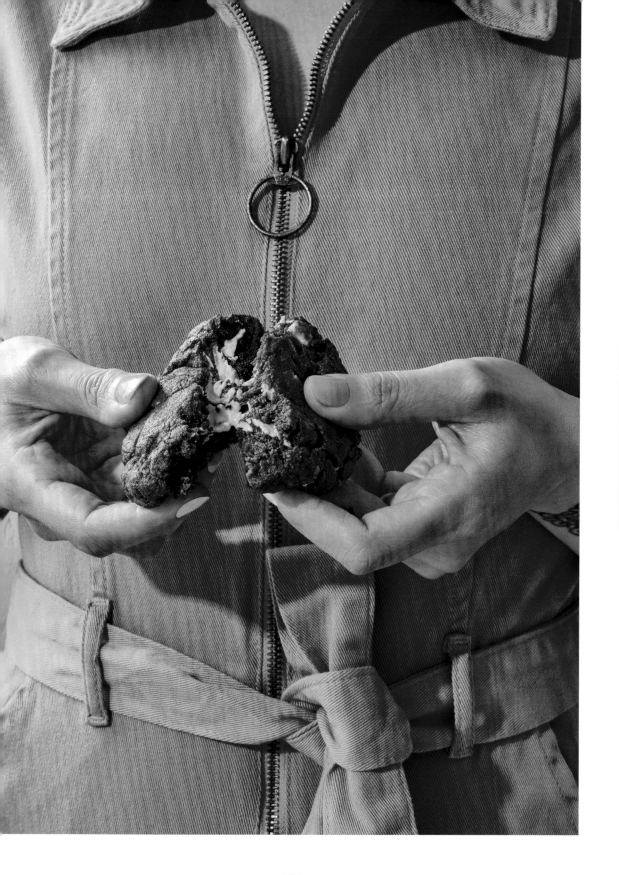

Makes 15-18

GINGER COOKIES
140g unsalted butter, softened
150g soft light brown sugar
70g golden syrup
1 egg

225g plain flour
1½ tsp bicarbonate of soda
2 tsp ground cinnamon
2 tsp ground ginger
¼ tsp ground cloves
150g demerara sugar

CREAM CHEESE ICING
70g unsalted butter, softened
a pinch of sea salt
115g cream cheese, at room temperature
395g icing sugar, sifted

GINGER CREAMS

A while back, Nikki made these Ginger Creams and brought them in for everyone as a treat, resulting in days of 'are there any more of those cookies?' and weeks of 'when are you making those cookies again?'. Just spicy enough, soft with a slightly crunchy bite, thanks to the demerara sugar, and filled with smooth cream cheese icing, these sandwich cookies will make you forget all about the ones at the supermarket.

FOR THE GINGER COOKIES
In a large bowl, bring together the butter, light brown sugar and golden syrup with a spatula or an electric hand mixer until well combined. Add the egg and and mix through until smooth, then add all of the dry ingredients, except for the demerara sugar, and fold through until you have a soft, squishy dough. Cover and place in the fridge for around 1 hour to firm up.

Preheat your oven to 190°C (170°C fan) and line a baking sheet with greaseproof paper.

Weigh out 20g nuggets of the dough and roll between your hands to make neat balls. Roll each one in the demerara sugar to completely coat them. Pop them onto the baking sheet 10cm/4in apart, to allow for spreading.

Bake for 10 minutes, then leave to cool down completely.

FOR THE CREAM CHEESE ICING
In a stand mixer fitted with the paddle attachment, or in a medium mixing bowl, beat together the butter and salt until pale and whippy. Add the cream cheese and beat together on a high speed for 1-2 minutes. Add the icing sugar in two stages, beating for a couple of minutes after each addition until you have a light, smooth, luxurious icing. Pop this into a piping bag fitted with a large round nozzle.

TO FINISH
Pair up the cookies and turn half of them over, ready to fill.

Pipe 5-6 small blobs of icing (about the size of a 50p piece) around the middle of the cookies, 1cm/½in from the edge. Place the other cookies on top and gently press down to allow the icing blobs to spread a bit and reach the edges of the sandwich. Place in the fridge until you're ready to eat.

TEAM TIP
Putting them in the fridge for a while will help the icing firm up. Actually, we all prefer them the day after they've been in the fridge overnight!

Cookies

Makes 12

230g unsalted butter,
  fridge-cold and cubed
160g soft light brown sugar

100g caster sugar
200g Caramelised White
  Chocolate (page 54),
  chopped into chunks
200g white chocolate chips

50g colourful sprinkles
  (strands/jimmies)
400g plain flour
100g self-raising flour

1 tsp sea salt
2 tsp baking powder
2 eggs plus 1 egg yolk
1 tsp vanilla extract

BIRTHDAY CAKE NY COOKIES

Pleasingly vanilla-y, full of oozing chunks of caramelised white chocolate and dotted with colourful rainbow sprinkles, these cookies bring bags of joy whether it's your birthday or not! We sell so many of these that we had to buy the biggest sous vide going in order to make the tonnes of caramelised white chocolate that go into them!

STAGE 1: BALLING

In the bowl of a stand mixer fitted with the paddle attachment, or by hand in a mixing bowl, beat the cold cubes of butter for a few seconds to break them up. Add the sugars and mix for 30-45 seconds until nuggets begin to form. Next, add the caramelised white chocolate chunks, chocolate chips and colourful sprinkles and mix a little, just to combine, before adding the flours, salt and baking powder. Stir until the mixture starts to look sandy but still has small nuggets of butter visible.

Whisk the eggs and yolk together with the vanilla in a separate bowl, then pour into the mixture and stir briefly until you end up with a chunky, nuggety dough. Be careful not to overmix it.

Tip it out onto a clean work surface and measure out 125g amounts, then squeeze each gently into a ball. Resist the urge to roll them.

Put the balls into an airtight container and freeze for at least 2 hours, ideally overnight.

STAGE 2: BAKING

Preheat your oven to 210°C (190°C fan) and line a baking sheet with greaseproof paper.

Remove the number of cookie balls you'd like to bake from the freezer and put them onto the baking sheet, spaced about 10cm/4in apart, as they will spread. Bake for 16 minutes until the tops are golden and the centres are soft and gooey.

Remove from the oven and allow to cool for at least 20 minutes.

Keep unused balls in the freezer for emergencies!

Cookies

185

Makes 1 x 15cm/6in cookie to serve 2

55g unsalted butter
65g soft light brown sugar
30g lightly whisked egg (this is around ½ large egg)
½ tsp vanilla extract
75g plain flour
¼ tsp sea salt
¼ tsp baking powder
⅛ tsp bicarbonate of soda
75g chocolate chips (we like a mix of milk and dark)
flaky sea salt, for topping
vanilla ice cream, to serve

SKILLET COOKIE

What's better than a warm, just-baked cookie? A giant cookie that is so chocolatey and gooey you need to eat it with a spoon! You can pick up little cast-iron frying pans for not very much money and I highly recommend you do, as they hold the heat beautifully and will give your skillet cookie that classic crispy outer crust. Serve with a scoop of ice cream for ultimate indulgence.

Preheat your oven to 200°C (180°C fan).

Heat a 15cm/6in cast-iron skillet over a high heat. Add the butter and melt, stirring frequently until it's giving off a delicious nutty aroma and has little brown flecks appearing at the bottom. Remove the skillet from the heat and transfer the burnt butter to a small bowl, allowing it to cool for 5 minutes.

Add the sugar, egg and vanilla to the bowl and stir through with a spoon or spatula. Add the flour, salt, baking powder and bicarb and stir to combine, then add two-thirds of the chocolate chips to the dough and stir until evenly distributed.

Transfer the dough to the skillet and press it out to an even layer, then sprinkle the remaining chocolate chips on top. Bake in the oven for 10 minutes.

Remove from the oven and let cool for 5-10 minutes, then sprinkle with flaky sea salt before plopping a generous scoop of ice cream into the middle and serving.

TEAM TIP
If you don't have a cast-iron skillet, you can make this in a small baking dish or even a cake tin. Just burn the butter in a saucepan at the beginning, mix all the ingredients in a bowl, then press into your dish or tin before baking as instructed above.

Makes 12

12 tbsp Biscoff spread,
  for the filling
230g unsalted butter,
  fridge-cold and cubed

160g soft light brown
  sugar
160g caster sugar
200g Caramelised White
  Chocolate (page 54),
  cut into chunks

200g white chocolate chips
100g mixed peel
100g crystallised ginger,
  finely chopped
2 tsp ground ginger
2 tsp ground cinnamon

½ tsp ground nutmeg
300g plain flour
200g self-raising flour
2 tsp baking powder
1 tsp sea salt
2 eggs plus 1 egg yolk

GINGER & BISCOFF NY COOKIES

I'm not entirely sure that these weren't invented so that Sam could order bags of crystallised ginger by the tonne. He's addicted to the stuff, and it gives these cookies a delicious warmth and sweetness. We originally came up with them as a Christmas special, but once the festivities were over we couldn't bear to take them off the menu. Here they are, in all their Biscoff and gingery glory, for you to enjoy all year round!

STAGE 1: FREEZING THE FILLING
Line a small tray with greaseproof paper. Spoon 12 tablespoon-sized blobs of Biscoff spread onto the tray and encourage them to be as round as possible (with your spoon, but feel free to encourage them verbally as well). You can also use a silicone truffle mould, if you have one, for maximum neatness! Pop the blobs into the freezer and freeze for at least at least 1 hour until they are as solid as a rock! Keep them in there until your cookie dough is ready to be balled.

STAGE 2: BALLING
Follow the instructions on page 184 for mixing your cookie dough, adding the mixed peel, crystallised ginger and the chocolate chunks along with the chocolate chips, and adding the spices with the flours.

Tip the dough out onto the work surface, then remove your frozen Biscoff blobs from the freezer. Using digital scales, weigh out 125g amounts of dough. Take a piece of unshaped cookie dough in one hand and push a frozen Biscoff blob into the centre, using your hands to wrap the cookie dough around it to enclose it completely. Repeat with the remaining dough and filling.

Pop the filled balls onto a tray and freeze for a minimum of 2 hours, but preferably overnight.

STAGE 3: BAKING
Preheat your oven to 210°C (190°C fan). Line a baking sheet with greaseproof paper.

Remove the number of cookie balls you'd like to bake from the freezer and put them onto the baking sheet, spaced about 10cm/4in apart, as they will spread. Bake for 16 minutes until the outer shell of each cookie is golden and cracked and the inside is soft and gooey.

Remove from the oven and allow to cool for 20 minutes before eating.

Makes 20

PREP
½ x batch of Cookie
   Dough (page 66)
½ x batch of Chocolate
   Cream Cheese Icing
   (page 38)

COOKIES
175g plain flour, sifted
½ tsp bicarbonate
   of soda
¼ tsp sea salt
115g unsalted
   butter, softened
50g caster sugar
110g soft light brown sugar
30g lightly whisked egg
   (½ large egg)
1 tsp vanilla extract
75g milk chocolate chips

COOKIE DOUGH COOKIES

What came first? The cookie or the cookie dough? It doesn't really matter when you can eat them at the same time! Using a nugget of soft cookie dough as the filling, and mouth-watering chocolate cream cheese icing to stick it all together, these little guys are the perfect things for cookie dough nibblers everywhere.

———

Make the Cookie Dough (page 66) and Chocolate Cream Cheese Icing (page 38) as directed and set aside.

FOR THE COOKIES
Preheat your oven to 190°C (170°C fan) and line two baking sheets with greaseproof paper.

Put the flour, bicarb and salt into a bowl, give it a little whisk and set aside.

In the bowl of a stand mixer fitted with the paddle attachment, or a large mixing bowl, slowly beat the butter and sugars together until well combined. Add the egg and vanilla, and briefly beat until smooth. Add the dry ingredients and fold through on a low speed or just with a spatula. Add the chocolate chips and fold through until evenly distributed. You should have a soft, squishy dough.

Get your digital scales out and weigh out 15g blobs of the dough. Roll them between your hands to make neat balls. Pop them onto the prepared baking sheets about 5cm/2in apart to allow for spreading.

Bake for 7–8 minutes until the cookies are slightly golden around the edges. Remove and allow to cool completely.

TO FINISH
Pair up the cookies and turn half of them over to be filled.

Take the pre-made cookie dough out of the freezer and chop it into 1cm/½in cubes, placing each onto a piece of greaseproof paper so they don't stick as they thaw.

Place your chocolate cream cheese icing into a piping bag with a medium round nozzle (or snip about 1cm/½in off the tip of the bag) and pipe a little ring of icing about 5mm/¼in from the edge of each cookie. Fill the hole in the centre with a little chunk of cookie dough. Top with the other cookie in the pair and squeeze gently so that the icing spreads to the edges of the sandwich.

Repeat until you have a glut of ridiculously cute and absurdly delicious sandwiches.

Cookies

Makes 12

PREP
2 x batches of Crumble Pie Crumb (page 64)

APPLE SAUCE FILLING
300g Bramley apples, peeled, cored, chopped into 1cm/½in chunks

100g unsalted butter
100g soft dark brown sugar
2 tsp ground cinnamon

COOKIE DOUGH
230g unsalted butter, fridge-cold and cubed

160g soft light brown sugar
160g caster sugar
200g Caramelised White Chocolate (page 54), cut into chunks
200g white chocolate chips

500g plain flour
2 tsp baking powder
1 tsp sea salt
1 tsp ground cinnamon
50g Crumble Pie Crumb, plus extra for coating (see Prep)
2 eggs

APPLE CRUMBLE NY COOKIES

Nikki came up with this gem during a flurry of product development a while back. It has all the familiar trappings of an apple crumble, from the intensely appley, cinnamon-spiced filling to the crumbly, crispy coating. For the ultimate indulgence, try one straight from the oven, with hot custard and vanilla ice cream!

———

Make the Crumble Pie Crumb as directed on page 64 and set aside.

STAGE 1: FREEZING THE FILLING
Bring all of the apple sauce ingredients to the boil in a small pan over a medium heat. Reduce to a simmer, cover and cook for about 5 minutes, stirring occasionally, until the apples have completely softened. Smoosh the apples to break them up a bit so you are left with a slightly chunky apple sauce. Leave to cool before putting in the fridge to chill for 2 hours.

Spoon 12 tablespoonfuls of the cold sauce onto a tray lined with greaseproof paper and shape them into individual balls with the spoon. If you have a silicone truffle mould, this is ideal to use instead! Freeze for at least 1 hour until hardened.

STAGE 2: BALLING
Follow the instructions on page 184 for mixing your cookie dough, adding the cinnamon and crumble pie crumb along with the flour, baking powder and salt.

Tip the dough onto the work surface and remove the apple sauce balls from the freezer. Using digital scales, weigh out 125g amounts of dough. Take a piece of unshaped dough in one hand and push a frozen apple sauce ball into the centre, wrapping the dough around it to enclose it completely. Repeat with the remaining dough and filling.

Tip the extra crumble pie crumb for coating into a bowl and toss each dough ball in it, pressing the crumbs all over the surface of the dough. Place the balls on a tray and freeze for at least 2 hours, ideally overnight.

STAGE 3: BAKING
Preheat your oven to 210°C (190°C fan). Line a baking sheet with greaseproof paper.

Remove the cookie balls from the freezer and place them on the baking sheet, spaced about 10cm/4in apart. Bake for 16 minutes until the outsides are golden and crumbly and the insides soft and gooey.

Remove from the oven and allow to cool for 20 minutes before eating. The apple sauce in the middle gets HOT!

Makes 12

COOKIES
100g caster sugar
100g soft light
 brown sugar
120g sunflower oil
75g water
1 tsp vanilla extract
300g plain flour
¼ tsp ground cinnamon
¾ tsp bicarbonate
 of soda
1 tsp baking powder
½ tsp sea salt

BISCOFF BUTTERCREAM
100g plant-based butter
 alternative
a pinch of sea salt
200g icing sugar, sifted
1 tbsp plant-based milk
40g Lotus Biscoff spread

TO FINISH
100–150g Lotus
 Biscoff spread
225g dark chocolate
 (54% cocoa solids)
½ tsp cocoa butter, melted
2–3 Lotus Biscoff biscuits,
 crushed

VEGAN BISCOFF SANDWICH COOKIES

Biscoff is one of those ingredients that is 'accidentally vegan', so it makes a brilliant addition to plant-based bakes. The cinnamon and brown sugar cookies are soft and slightly chewy, and once they are sandwiched together with Biscoff buttercream and a pool of oozing biscuit spread, then dipped in chocolate, they become totally irresistible.

FOR THE COOKIES

In a medium bowl, whisk together the sugars, sunflower oil, water and vanilla until just combined. Add the flour, cinnamon, bicarb, baking powder and salt, and fold through the mixture with a spatula until you have a smooth, paste-like dough. Cover and refrigerate for at least 1 hour or overnight.

Preheat your oven to 190°C (170°C fan) and line 2 baking sheets with greaseproof paper.

Scoop out 30g amounts of the dough (use those scales!) and roll them into balls. Place on a tray and freeze for around 10 minutes.

Pop the thoroughly chilled balls onto the prepared baking sheets and bake for 12–15 minutes until the tops are lovely and golden. Remove from the oven and leave to cool completely.

FOR THE BISCOFF BUTTERCREAM

In a medium bowl, whip the plant-based butter and salt with an electric hand mixer until light and fluffy. Add the icing sugar in two stages, beating for a few minutes after each addition. Loosen the mixture to the right consistency by adding your plant-based milk a little at a time. Beat until whippy and smooth, then mix in the Biscoff spread until well combined. Transfer to a piping bag.

TO FINISH

Pair up your cookies and turn one half of them upside down for filling. Pipe a ring of the buttercream about 1cm/½in from the outside of the cookie and fill the centre with a heaped teaspoon of Biscoff spread. Pop the top cookies on and press them down slightly to encourage the buttercream to spread to the edges. Place the sandwiches into the fridge for 20 minutes or so.

Line a baking sheet with greaseproof paper.

Melt the chocolate with the cocoa butter, either over a bain-marie or in the microwave in short bursts. Plunge half of each cookie into the runny chocolate and allow the excess to dribble off. Place each cookie onto the greaseproof paper, sprinkle with the Biscoff biscuit crumbs and leave to set before eating.

Makes 18

FOR THE SALTED CARAMEL FILLINGS
1 x batch of Salted Caramel (page 42)
100g unsalted butter, softened
160g icing sugar, sifted

FOR THE CRACKLE COOKIES
125g unsalted butter, softened
300g soft light brown sugar
2 eggs
1 tsp vanilla extract
150g plain flour
50g cocoa powder

2 tsp baking powder
a pinch of sea salt
225g dark chocolate chips (70% cocoa solids), melted and cooled slightly
3 tbsp milk
100g crunchy pretzels

TO FINISH
1 x batch of Dark Chocolate Ganache (page 52), cooled to a spreadable consistency (see method)

CARAMEL PRETZEL COOKIE SARNIES

Chocolate Crackle Cookies were already a huge hit in the shop, but the first time we took two and sandwiched them together with salted caramel buttercream, chocolate ganache and oozing caramel, we knew we could never go back! If you're pushed for time, the cookies are great on their own but if you want to do like we do, you'll throw everything at them, including smashed pretzels for added crunch.

FOR THE SALTED CARAMEL FILLINGS
Make the Salted Caramel as directed on page 42 and allow to cool.

In the bowl of a stand mixer fitted with the paddle attachment, or a medium mixing bowl, beat the butter on a high speed for 5 minutes until it has turned very pale and whippy. Add the icing sugar in two stages, beating for 3-5 minutes after each addition. Add 3 tablespoons of the salted caramel, adding more to taste, and beat it into the buttercream for 3 minutes. Taste and add extra salt if you feel it needs it.

Cover the remaining salted caramel and pop it back in the fridge. Cover the buttercream and leave it at room temperature for later.

FOR THE CRACKLE COOKIES
In the bowl of a stand mixer fitted with the paddle attachment, or a large mixing bowl, beat together the butter and sugar until light and fluffy. Beat in the eggs, one at a time, then mix in the vanilla.

In a separate bowl, sift together the flour, cocoa, baking powder and salt, then add to the wet ingredients and fold through. Fold in the cooled, melted chocolate and finally the milk until all the ingredients are well combined and you have a fairly wet dough. Cover the bowl and pop it into the fridge for about 1 hour.

Preheat your oven to 190°C (170°C fan) and line 2 baking sheets with greaseproof paper.

Measure out 25g nuggets of dough and roll them into balls, placing them 10cm/4in apart on the baking sheets to allow for spreading. Place a pretzel on top of each of the balls, pressing them down slightly. Bake for 12 minutes, then remove from the oven and leave to cool completely.

Meanwhile, make your Dark Chocolate Ganache as directed on page 52, so that it has time to set to a spreadable consistency.   >

Cookies

197

< TO FINISH

Match up pairs of cookies and turn one half of each pair upside down for filling.

Fill three piping bags: one with the ganache, one with the buttercream and one with the the remaining salted caramel.

Pipe a ring of ganache onto the upturned cookies. Top that with a ring of buttercream, then fill the hole with the caramel. Pop the top cookie on to make a sandwich and give it a light press so that the fillings spread all the way to the edge. Crush up the remaining pretzels and push them into the sides of the cookies where the filling has smooshed out, completely covering the band of buttercream and ganache.

TEAM TIP

These are best when they have been in the fridge for a little while and set nicely. Not only does the cookie become even more fudgy, you will avoid sullying your shirt with blobs of escaped filling when you bite into them!

Cookies

Makes 13

CHOCOLATE BISCUITS
225g unsalted butter, softened
150g caster sugar
50g soft light brown sugar
1 egg
1 tsp vanilla extract
350g plain flour, plus extra for dusting
50g cocoa powder
1 tsp sea salt
½ tsp bicarbonate of soda

MARSHMALLOW FILLING
12g powdered gelatine
60g plus 30g water
90g plus 90g liquid glucose
75g caster sugar
1 tsp vanilla extract

TO FINISH
100g seedless raspberry jam
180g good-quality milk chocolate (at least 50% cocoa solids)

MALLOW WHEELS

The best part of my packed lunch at school was, naturally, the chocolate biscuit and there was one marshmallow-filled, chocolate-coated one that I would cross my fingers for every day. These Mallow Wheels are an upgraded version – crumbly chocolate cookies sandwiched together with flumpy homemade marshmallow and jam, then half-dunked in milk chocolate. You'll need to grin to get one in!

FOR THE CHOCOLATE BISCUITS

Preheat your oven to 190°C (170°C fan) and line 2 baking sheets with greaseproof paper.

In the bowl of a stand mixer fitted with the paddle attachment, or a mixing bowl, beat together the butter and sugars until slightly paler in colour. Add the egg and vanilla, and beat in until well combined. Sift in the flour, cocoa, salt and bicarb, stirring through on a low setting until you have a fairly soft dough. Wrap in greaseproof paper and chill for 15 minutes to allow it to firm up slightly.

To make your life easier, work on the dough in two halves. Take the first half and briefly knead it on the counter until you have a nice smooth ball. Lightly dust the work surface and a rolling pin with flour and roll out the dough gently, turning frequently and re-dusting underneath whenever it feels sticky. Aim for a thickness of 4mm/¼in all over. Chomp out circles with an 8cm/3¼in round cookie cutter, placing them carefully onto the prepared baking sheets a couple of centimetres apart.

Bake for 14–16 minutes until cooked through and crisp at the edges. Leave to cool and repeat with any unused dough (see Tip).

FOR THE MARSHMALLOW FILLING

In a small bowl, combine the powdered gelatine with 60g of water, stir briefly and leave for 5–10 minutes until it has jellified.

Pop the jellified disc into the microwave for 30 seconds to melt it, then pour it into the bowl of a stand mixer fitted with the balloon whisk attachment. Add 90g of liquid glucose and get it mixing on a low speed to keep the mixture moving while you prepare the sugar syrup.

Put the remaining 90g of liquid glucose, 30g of water and the sugar into a small saucepan and set over a low-medium heat with a thermometer inside the pan, stirring once or twice to combine. Let the syrup bubble away for a few minutes until the thermometer reads anywhere between 112–115°C, then remove from the heat.   >

< With the whisk still running, add the sugar syrup to the gelatine mixture in a slow, steady stream, down the inside of the bowl. Once all of the sugar syrup is in, turn the mixer speed to medium and whisk for 5 minutes. It should still be quite runny at this stage. Increase the speed to high and whisk for a further 5 minutes. It should now be lovely and thick but still run slowly off the whisk when you remove it. Add the vanilla and put it back on a high speed for a final 2-5 minutes until it hold stiff peaks.

TO FINISH

While you are making your marshmallow, pair up your cookies and turn one in each pair upside down for filling. Place the jam in a piping bag (it's a good idea to whisk or even blend the jam first to smooth out any lumps and prevent it clogging up the piping bag) and snip the end off. Lastly, get a large piping bag ready, fitted with a large round nozzle.

When the marshmallow is ready, work quickly as it will begin to set. Pop the lot into the prepared piping bag. Working on two biscuits at a time, pipe a generous blob of marshmallow onto the centre of the upturned cookies. Poke the end of the jammy piping bag into the middle of the blob and squeeze in a little jam until you can see the marshmallow swelling a bit. Put the other biscuit on top immediately and push down so that the marshmallow spreads out to reach the edges of the sandwich. Continue with the rest of the biscuits.

Prepare a baking sheet or two with silpats or greaseproof paper. Melt the chocolate in a small bowl, either over a bain-marie or gently in the microwave in 15-second bursts. Dip one half of each mallow wheel into the chocolate, allowing the excess to dribble back into the bowl. Place them on the baking sheet and allow to set.

——

TEAM TIP

If you would like to save some biscuit dough for another time, make a fat disc of dough, wrap it in clingfilm and store in the fridge. When you're ready to bake, take the dough out 20 minutes before you roll it, then carry on as normal.

Makes 14

SHORTBREAD BISCUITS
75g unsalted butter,
  softened
30g caster sugar
½ tsp vanilla extract

115g plain flour, plus
  extra for dusting
½ tsp sea salt

**CHEWY CARAMEL
FILLING**
90g double cream

¼ tsp vanilla extract
¼ tsp sea salt
90g golden syrup
105g caster sugar
30g unsalted butter,
  cold and cubed

TOPPING
100g good-quality
  milk chocolate
  (at least 33%
  cocoa solids)

TWICKS BITES

Like a millionaire's shortbread, but bite-sized, these little morsels are surprisingly simple to make and they contain everything I want from a great bake. They're salty, sweet, chewy, crumbly and chocolatey, and they might actually be my favourite new bake in this book. There... I said it!

——

FOR THE SHORTBREAD BISCUITS
Preheat your oven to 190°C (170°C fan) and line two baking sheets with greaseproof paper.

In a medium bowl, mix the butter, sugar and vanilla with a wooden spoon until combined. Add the flour and salt and stir together to form clumpy breadcrumbs. Squeeze the mixture together in the bowl using your hands, then turn it out onto the work surface, kneading briefly until the dough is smooth.

Dust the work surface and a rolling pin with flour and roll out the dough to a 5mm/¼in thick disc, turning frequently and carefully, re-dusting the surface and the rolling pin whenever it feels like it might stick. The dough might crack as you roll – just squeeze it back together with your hands and keep rolling. Chomp out circles using a 5cm/2in round cookie cutter and

place them onto the baking sheet 2cm/¾in apart. Bake for 10 minutes until the tops are lightly golden and the underside of each cookie is cooked.

Remove from the oven and, while they're still hot, gently press into the centre of each cookie using something round and flat that is 2.5cm in diameter (I use the bottom of a small shot glass or a small cake decorating rolling pin). You need to be careful not to press so hard that the biscuit cracks up. You are only trying to make a light indentation for the caramel to sit in. Leave to cool.

FOR THE CHEWY CARAMEL FILLING
Mix together the cream, vanilla and salt in a small jug and set nearby.

In a medium saucepan with a sugar thermometer inside, heat the golden syrup and sugar over a medium heat, stirring occasionally. Once the mixture has reached 155°C, remove from the heat and pour in the cream mixture, a little at a time, stirring quickly and carefully until all of the cream has been incorporated.

Return to a medium heat and allow it to bubble away until it reaches 127°C, then remove from the heat again and   >

<   add the butter, stirring until it's all melted and combined.

TO FINISH

While the caramel is still hot (and I mean hot, so do be careful), spoon out just over a teaspoon directly from the pan and blob it right into the middle of each biscuit using the indentation as a guide. This will also go some way to containing the caramel, but add more if you want, just know that it will creep towards the edges of the biscuits eventually! Leave to cool down completely.

Melt the chocolate in a small bowl, either over a bain-marie or gently in the microwave in 15-second bursts. While it's still warm, dunk each biscuit, caramel-side down, into the chocolate and allow any excess to dribble off.

Set the biscuit, right-side up, on a cooling rack or baking sheet lined with greaseproof paper. Before they have a chance to set, press a fork lightly into the top of each biscuit to create a little ripple effect in the chocolate top. Leave to set completely.

Makes about 22

PREP
½ x batch of Biscoff
   Swiss Meringue
   Buttercream (page 40)

SPICED COOKIE CUPS
55g unsalted butter,
   softened
95g soft light brown sugar
½ large egg (see Tip)
½ tsp vanilla extract
125g plain flour, plus
   extra for dusting

¼ tsp ground cinnamon
¼ tsp sea salt
¼ tsp bicarbonate of
   soda

**BISCOFF CHEESECAKE
FILLING**
145g cream cheese

½ large egg (see Tip)
30g caster sugar
50g Lotus Biscoff spread

TO DECORATE
50g Lotus Biscoff spread
10 Lotus Biscoff biscuits,
   broken into small pieces

BISCOFF COOKIE CUPS

I first made cookie cups for the Cupcake Jemma channel by baking a cupcake inside a cookie. It was great, but enter team Crumbs who ditched my cupcake filling and replaced it with cheesecake! At first, I was a little put out, but oh jeez were they right. The tangy, soft filling, flavoured with everyone's favourite biscuit spread, is the perfect match for the crisp but yielding cookie cup. We ice these like a cupcake and they are totes adorbs. Down in one!

———

Make the Biscoff Swiss Meringue Buttercream as directed on page 40, cover and set aside.

FOR THE COOKIE CUPS
Lightly grease a 24-hole mini cupcake tin.

In the bowl of a stand mixer fitted with the paddle attachment, or a medium bowl, cream together the butter and sugar for 30 seconds, just to combine. Add the egg and vanilla and beat until combined. Sift in the flour, cinnamon, salt and bicarb, and fold for a few seconds until well distributed and you have a soft, squishy dough.

Use digital scales to weigh out 15g nuggets of the dough and roll them into little balls. Pop one into each of the holes of the tin.

Using a flat-bottomed implement about 2.5cm/1in thick, such as a mini rolling pin, press down on top of each ball, allowing the dough to travel up the sides of the tin to the top. If it's sticking, dust it with flour every now and then. Pop the tin into the fridge while you make the cheesecake filling.

FOR THE BISCOFF CHEESECAKE FILLING
Preheat your oven to 190°C (170°C fan).

Put all the filling ingredients into a stand mixer fitted with the balloon whisk, or a medium bowl, and whisk together for 5 minutes or so until the mixture is light and whippy, then transfer the mixture to a piping bag.

Fill each cookie cup with the mixture, then bake for 10 minutes until the cookies are golden.

Remove from the oven and leave to cool for 15–20 minutes, then remove them carefully from the tin and allow to cool completely. Taking them out too soon may cause the rims to break off.   >

<   TO FINISH

Put your Biscoff buttercream into a piping bag fitted with a round nozzle, then pipe chubby blobs of buttercream on top of each cookie cup. Put them all onto a tray and refrigerate for 15 minutes.

Meanwhile, warm the Biscoff spread in the microwave and put it into a small bowl.

When the buttercream on top of the cookie cups has chilled and firmed up a bit, remove the cups from the fridge and, one by one, dip them blob-first into the bowl of Biscoff spread, allowing the excess to dribble off.

Finish each cookie cup off with a little piece of Lotus biscuit to decorate.

TEAM TIP

Occasionally, a recipe calls for half an egg, as it does here. To split your egg in half, a knife won't cut it, literally. Crack your egg and whisk it, then use a set of scales to weigh it. Divide that weight in two and transfer half to a separate bowl.

CAKES

CAKES

Now it's time to get serious! But not too serious. At Crumbs & Doilies, cake is King and the very best of what we do. While some of the cakes in this chapter are what we would describe as 'project cakes', they are all fun to make, a great opportunity to play around with flavours, textures and decoration, and – best of all – they taste amazing!

It probably goes without saying that making a 4- or 8-layer cake will take a little time and effort, and some of the recipes in this chapter will require you to make up to 8 different elements! But don't let that put you off, because there is a trick to successfully constructing a knockout layer cake and that is preparation. To help you to get yourself ready, each recipe begins with the different elements you will need so that you can get prepped, to ensure there isn't a panic as assembly time approaches.

You'll find detailed descriptions in each recipe for how to decorate your cakes just like we do in the bakery. However, never forget these are your cakes and you can dress them up however you like. Either way, we want you to have the confidence and skills to make and decorate your cakes like a pro, so check out the QR codes below, which will show you multiple techniques to get you started.

Splitting a sponge

Filling a cake

Trimming and levelling

Crumb-coating

How to drip

Cutting a cake

BIRTHDAY CAKE 212

VELVET VOLCANO CAKE 215

END OF THE WORLD CHOCOLATE CAKE 218

TIRAMISU CAKE 221

RASPBERRY & YUZU CAKE 224

HONEY CRUNCHY NUT CAKE 227

S'MORES CAKE 230

MATCHA & BLACK SESAME CAKE 233

FERRERO ROCHER CAKE 236

STICKY TOFFEE CAKE 239

LEMON MESS CAKE 242

SALTED CARAMEL CAKE 245

RASPBERRY, PISTACHIO & CHOCOLATE CAKE 248

MARATHON CAKE 251

BLUEBERRY CHEESECAKE 254

COOKIE DOUGH CAKE 257

CAKE BALLS 260

Makes 1 x 20cm/8in
cake to serve 12-16

PREP
2 x batches of Vanilla
 Buttercream (page 36)

VANILLA FUNFETTI
SPONGE
500g caster sugar
135g vegetable oil
330g unsalted
 butter, softened
8 eggs
500g self-raising flour
80g rainbow sprinkles
6 tbsp milk
1½ tsp vanilla extract

RAINBOW POOPS
70g egg whites
140g caster sugar
⅛ tsp cream of tartar
a pinch of sea salt
⅛ tsp vanilla extract
 (optional)
food colouring paste in
 red, orange, yellow,
 green, blue and purple

TO FINISH
½ jar of raspberry
 or strawberry jam
rainbow sprinkles

BIRTHDAY CAKE

When I think of birthday cake, I never really think about any flavour other than vanilla. It must be a light, moist sponge, intensely vanilla-y, filled and decorated with vanilla buttercream, not fondant, and it 100% has to have raspberry jam in the middle. The only way you could make that kind of cake better, in my opinion, is to add colourful sprinkles to the sponge and rainbow meringue poops to the top. This cake is the epitome of birthday cuteness!

———

Make the Vanilla Buttercream as directed on page 36 and set aside.

FOR THE FUNFETTI SPONGE
Preheat your oven to 190°C (170°C fan) and grease four 20cm/8in round sandwich tins.

In the bowl of a stand mixer fitted with the paddle attachment, or a large mixing bowl, beat together the sugar, vegetable oil and butter on a medium–high speed for a couple of minutes until light and fluffy. Add the eggs, two at a time, beating for 30 seconds after each addition to make sure they're well incorporated. Sift the flour directly into the bowl, then add the colourful sprinkles. Fold through on the lowest speed of the mixer, or by hand with a large metal spoon or rubber spatula. When almost all of the flour has been incorporated, add the milk and vanilla, and fold gently until completely combined.

Distribute the batter among the prepared tins and level the tops with a palette knife.

Bake for 22–24 minutes, or until a skewer inserted into the middle of each sponge comes out clean. Leave to cool for 15–20 minutes before removing from the tins and allowing to cool completely.

FOR THE RAINBOW POOPS
Reduce the oven to 120°C (100°C fan) and line a baking sheet with greaseproof paper.

Prepare a French meringue mixture as directed on page 45.

Meanwhile, prepare a large piping bag fitted with a big round nozzle. Dab a pea-sized blob of each colour paste onto a plate leaving some space between each. Have a glass of clean water nearby. Loosen the paste with a tiny amount of water. This will make it easier to paint on and make the colour less concentrated. Using a clean brush for each colour, paint up the inside of the piping bag, being careful not to overlap colours or allow them to touch each other inside. We like   >

< to get more coverage by doing two rounds of each colour in the bag, but if you want a bit more of the white meringue to show, one stripe of each will be fine. Head to the QR code on page 24 to see how we do it.

Empty all of the meringue into the piping bag and squeeze out the first bit to make sure the colours are coming through (you can use these first blobs to stick the greaseproof paper to the baking sheet!). Pipe neat, colourful blobs onto the greaseproof paper.

Bake for 1 hour, then turn the oven off and allow the poops to cool slowly inside.

TO FINISH

Level and trim your sponges (see QR code on page 210) and stick the first layer onto a cake board or a large, flat plate using a little bit of vanilla buttercream.

Using an offset palette knife, spread a generous, even layer of vanilla buttercream all over the sponge. With the palette knife set about 2.5cm/1in in from the outside edge, scrape off some of the buttercream to create a shallow divot (it should look like a side plate). Fill the hollow with a thin layer of jam and level it out with a palette knife.

Repeat the above step for the next two sponge layers. Finish with the final layer of sponge upside-down for a neat top.

Crumb-coat the top and sides of the cake with vanilla buttercream (see QR code on page 210), then chill in the fridge for at least 30 minutes.

Once the icing is firm to the touch, remove from the fridge and give it a generous top coat of the buttercream, removing the excess as you smooth out the sides and top with a cake scraper or palette knife. Chill for another 10 minutes.

Take a small amount of the buttercream and colour it pink (or another colour if pink isn't your vibe). Using a small offset palette knife, apply a band of pink buttercream around the bottom half of the cake, smoothing it out with a cake scraper so that it sits a little proud of the rest of the cake.

Finish the top half of the cake with colourful sprinkles and blobs of white vanilla buttercream topped with the rainbow poops.

———

TEAM TIP

Don't put too much jam into the middle layers. Too much will make the layers slide about, making it very difficult to decorate and achieve nice straight sides.

Makes 1 x 20cm/8in
cake to serve 12-16

PREP
1 x batch of Oreo
  Buttercream (page 36)
1 x batch of Cream
  Cheese Icing (page 38)

1 x batch of Cookie
  Dough (page 66),
  cut into chunks
½ x batch of Salted
  Caramel (page 42)

RED VELVET SPONGE
250g buttermilk
½ tsp vanilla extract
1½ tsp red food
  colouring paste

250g unsalted butter,
  softened
600g caster sugar
6 eggs
25g cocoa powder
375g plain flour
½ tsp sea salt
1 tbsp cider vinegar
1 tsp bicarbonate
  of soda

TO FINISH
1 packet of Oreos:
  half broken into
  small pieces;
  half crushed to
  a fine crumb
1 x batch of Dark
  Chocolate Drip
  Ganache (page 52)

VELVET VOLCANO CAKE

The Big Daddy version of our famous Velvet Volcano Cupcake, this cake is an amalgamation of some of the best bits the C&D bakery has knocking about. It's one of my personal favourites, so it absolutely had to make it into the book. It features our soft, fluffy red velvet sponge sandwiched together with cream cheese icing, cookie dough chunks and decorated with Oreo buttercream, chocolate ganache and salted caramel.

Make your Oreo Buttercream (page 36), Cream Cheese Icing (page 38), Cookie Dough (page 66) and Salted Caramel (page 42), and set aside.

FOR THE RED VELVET SPONGE

Preheat your oven to 190°C (170°C fan) and grease four 20cm/8in round sandwich tins.

In a small jug, whisk together the buttermilk, vanilla and red food colouring until completely combined, then set aside.

In the bowl of a stand mixer fitted with the paddle attachment, or a large mixing bowl, beat together the butter and sugar on a medium speed for 2-4 minutes until very pale and fluffy. Add the eggs, two at

a time, beating well after each addition. Sift the cocoa, flour and salt directly into the bowl and fold in carefully using a large metal spoon or the lowest setting on the stand mixer. When the dry ingredients are about half mixed through, pour in the red buttermilk mixture and fold through.

In a very small bowl, combine the cider vinegar and bicarb, then quickly add it to the rest of the batter as it fizzes, folding it through gently until thoroughly combined.

Divide the batter evenly among your prepared tins, levelling the tops a little, then bake for 22-24 minutes until a skewer inserted into the middle of each sponge comes out clean.

Remove from the oven and leave to cool for 15-20 minutes before removing from the tins and allowing to cool completely.

TO FINISH

Level and trim your sponges (see QR code on page 210) and stick the first layer onto a cake board or a large, flat plate using a little bit of Oreo buttercream.

Layer up your cake, filling it with generous amounts of cream cheese icing, broken >

< Oreo cookies and chunks of cookie dough.

Crumb-coat the top and sides of the cake with the Oreo buttercream (see QR code on page 210), then chill in the fridge for at least 30 minutes, or until firm to the touch.

Remove your cake from the fridge and give it a generous top coat with the Oreo buttercream, removing the excess as you smooth out the sides and top with a cake scraper or palette knife.

Make the Chocolate Drip Ganache using the method on page 52, then put it into a piping bag. Carefully pipe large zigzags of ganache across the top of the cake, allowing some of it to drip down the sides.

Repeat the zigzags with the salted caramel, but this time go across at right angles to the ganache to create a criss-cross pattern and alternate drips down the sides of the cake.

Pile a generous amount of the remaining cream cheese icing on top of the cake, to create an organised mess, then stud this all over with pieces of cookie dough and chunks of Oreo cookies to finish.

Makes 1 x 20cm/8in
cake to serve 12-16

PREP
1 x batch of Chocolate
Pie Crumb (page 64)
1 x batch of Chocolate
Cream Cheese Icing
(page 38)

CHOCOLATE SPONGE
650g plain flour
690g caster sugar
120g cocoa powder
2 tsp bicarbonate of soda
1 tsp sea salt
6 eggs
450g buttermilk
450g brewed or instant
    coffee, cooled
390g vegetable oil

CHOCOLATE TRUFFLES
150g dark chocolate
    chips (54% cocoa
    solids)
15g unsalted butter,
    cold and cubed
60g double cream
cocoa powder, for
    dusting
gold leaf (optional)

CHOCOLATE SHARDS
100g dark chocolate
    chips (70% or
    50% cocoa solids)

TO FINISH
2 x batches of Buttery
    Ganache Icing
    (page 52)

END OF THE WORLD CHOCOLATE CAKE

Imagine if Bruce Bogtrotter was all grown up, he'd tidied himself up a bit, graduated, got himself a good job in a respectable company and was generally a whole lot classier than his 11-year-old self – but, he still had a penchant for extremely chocolatey chocolate cake. I think this elegant little number might just tickle his fancy.

———

Make the Chocolate Pie Crumb (page 64) and the Chocolate Cream Cheese Icing (page 38), cover and set aside.

FOR THE CHOCOLATE SPONGE
Preheat your oven to 190°C (170°C fan) and grease four 20cm/8in round sandwich tins.

In a medium bowl, whisk together the flour, sugar, cocoa, bicarb and salt.

In a separate, large mixing bowl, whisk together the eggs, buttermilk, cooled coffee and oil until combined, then add the dry ingredients to the wet and whisk until thoroughly combined so that you have a smooth, runny batter.

Distribute the batter evenly among the prepared tins, then bake for 24–30 minutes until a skewer inserted into the centre of each sponge comes out clean.

Leave to cool for 15–20 minutes before removing from the tins and allowing them to cool completely.

FOR THE CHOCOLATE TRUFFLES
Melt the chocolate and butter together, either over a bain-marie or gently in the microwave in 15-second bursts. Add the cream and stir to combine thoroughly. Pour this mixture into a small tray, bowl or dish and refrigerate until set.

Once set, remove from the fridge and use a couple of teaspoons to scoop out the mixture and roll between your palms to make beautiful round truffles.

Alternatively, if you have a truffle mould, fill it up with the truffle mixture, then leave the truffles in the fridge to set.

Toss half of the truffles in a bowl of cocoa to cover completely. Leave the remaining truffles plain or decorate them with   **>**

< gold leaf. Put the truffles in the fridge until you need them... and try hard not to eat them!

FOR THE CHOCOLATE SHARDS

Line a baking sheet with greaseproof paper or a silpat.

Melt the chocolate using the method on page 19, then pour it onto the baking sheet and spread it out with an offset palette knife to 2–3mm thick. Use the tip of the palette knife to make swooshy marks in the top of the chocolate. Leave for a minute or two until it's no longer wet but still a bit tacky, then use the back of a knife to score lines all across the chocolate sheet, criss-crossing them so that you have lots of pointy triangles of different sizes. Leave to set completely.

Once the scored sheet is set and snappy, break it apart along the score lines that you marked out to make lots of different-sized shards of chocolate. Set aside or store them in the fridge if they haven't set properly.

TO FINISH

Start by making the Buttery Ganache Icing as directed on page 52 so that it has time to set to a spreadable consistency.

Level and trim the sponges (see QR code on page 210), then stick the first layer onto a cake board or a large, flat plate using some chocolate cream cheese icing. Build up the cake layers filling them with generous helpings of the chocolate cream cheese icing and a sprinkling of chocolate pie crumb (see QR code on page 210).

Use the buttery ganache icing to crumb-coat the top and sides of the cake (see QR code on page 210) and chill for at least 30 minutes, or until the ganache is firm to the touch.

Apply a final neat top coat of buttery ganache all over the chilled cake, using a cake smoother or palette knife to make it as smooth as possible.

Whip the remaining buttery ganache with an electric or a balloon whisk until it is slightly paler in colour and a lovely mousse-like consistency. Use this to dollop on top of the cake with a spoon. You're aiming for organised chaos here, so don't make it too neat. Decorate with your truffles, chocolate shards and chocolate pie crumb – remember, this is a cake for the end of the world, so go nuts!

Makes 1 x 20cm/8in cake to serve 12-16

PREP
1 x batch of Vanilla
 Buttercream (page 36)
1 x batch of Espresso
 Buttercream (page 36)
½ x batch of Mascarpone
 Icing (page 38)

CHOCOLATE TRUFFLES
150g dark chocolate
 chips (54%
 cocoa solids)
15g unsalted butter
60g double cream
25g cocoa
 powder, sifted
1-2 tbsp cocoa powder

gold leaf or gold lustre
 dust (optional)

ESPRESSO SPONGE
500g caster sugar
330g unsalted butter,
 softened
135g vegetable oil
8 eggs
500g self-raising flour

6 tbsp espresso
 coffee, cooled
 (or strong instant)

TO FINISH
Marsala wine or
 espresso, for soaking
 the sponges
80g dark chocolate,
 melted and cooled

TIRAMISU CAKE

Tiramisu is such a respected dessert, but I'm confident this Tiramisu Cake will delight fans of the traditional Italian pud and hopefully everyone else as well! With its Marsala-soaked espresso sponges, espresso buttercream, fluffy mascarpone icing and classic dusting of cocoa powder, it's a favourite bake among staff and customers alike.

——

Make your Vanilla and Espresso Buttercreams (page 36) and Mascarpone Icing (page 38), cover and set aside.

FOR THE CHOCOLATE TRUFFLES

Melt together the chocolate and butter, either over a bain-marie or gently in the microwave in 15-second bursts, then add the cream and stir to combine thoroughly.

If you have a silicone truffle mould, pour the ganache mixture into the holes and place in the fridge to set. Otherwise, just put it into a bowl and refrigerate until set, then use a teaspoon to scoop small amounts out that you can roll between your hands (wear latex gloves to avoid heat transfer and very messy hands!). Place the balls onto a baking sheet lined with greaseproof paper and chill for at least 1 hour.

Once they're set, toss half of the truffles in the cocoa and leave the other half plain, or jazz them up with gold leaf or lustre if you fancy, then pop them back into the fridge until it's decorating time!

FOR THE ESPRESSO SPONGE

Preheat your oven to 190°C (170°C fan) and grease four 20cm/8in round sandwich tins.

In the bowl of a stand mixer fitted with the paddle attachment, or a large mixing bowl, beat together the sugar, butter and oil for a couple of minutes until pale and fluffy. Add the eggs, two at a time, beating for 30 seconds after each addition to ensure they are well combined. Sift the flour directly into the bowl and start to fold it through on the lowest speed of the mixer or by hand using a large metal spoon. When the flour is almost completely incorporated, pour in the cooled espresso and fold that in as well to create a thick, smooth batter.

Distribute the batter evenly among the prepared tins and level the tops with a palette knife.

Bake for 22-24 minutes, or until a skewer inserted into the centre of each sponge comes out clean.   >

< Leave to cool for 15–20 minutes before removing from the tins and allowing to cool completely.

TO FINISH
Level and trim your espresso sponges (see QR code on page 210) and use a cake leveller or a sharp, serrated bread knife to carefully split each sponge into two layers so that you have 8 thin, fragile layers. Stick the first layer onto a cake board or a large, flat plate using some espresso buttercream.

Drizzle or brush a small amount of Marsala or espresso all over the sponge. You want to lightly soak, not drown it! Top with a generous, even layer of mascarpone icing.

Place the next sponge layer on top and repeat, but this time with a layer of espresso buttercream.

Keep building up the layers in this way, alternating between the two icings and finishing with an upside-down sponge for the top layer. Chill in the fridge for at least 20 minutes, then trim any lumps and bumps off the edge of the cake with a serrated knife to neaten the sides.

Crumb-coat the top and sides of the cake with coffee buttercream (see QR code on page 210) and chill for 30 minutes, or until the icing is set.

Apply a neat top coat of vanilla buttercream and chill for another 10 minutes.

Take some of the remaining coffee buttercream and use a palette knife to spread a light band of it all around the bottom half of the cake. Smooth this out with a cake scraper and chill for 10 minutes until set.

Mix a little of the melted and cooled chocolate into some of the remaining vanilla buttercream and repeat the previous step, but this time only go about two-thirds of the way up the coffee band, to create a two-layer effect.

Pour the remaining melted chocolate into the centre of the top of the cake and spread it out with a small palette knife to create a pool of chocolate, leaving a 2.5cm/1in ring of exposed buttercream around the edge. Using a small sieve, carefully dust this with cocoa, taking care not to go over the exposed buttercream.

Put the last of the coffee buttercream into a piping bag fitted with a star nozzle, then pipe neat blobs, just over 2.5cm/1in apart, around the edge of the top of the cake.

Take your truffles from the fridge and place them alternately in between the buttercream blobs to finish.

223

Makes 1 x 20cm/8in cake to serve 12-16

PREP
1 x batch of Raspberry Goo (page 60)
1 x batch of Raspberry Buttercream (page 36)
1 x batch of Yuzu Buttercream (page 36)
1 x batch of Yuzu Curd (page 58)

RASPBERRY RIPPLE SPONGE
500g caster sugar
330g unsalted butter
135g vegetable oil
8 eggs
500g self-raising flour
6 tbsp milk
1 tsp vanilla extract
6-8 tbsp Raspberry Goo (see Prep)

WHITE CHOCOLATE DISCS
50g white chocolate chips
5g freeze-dried raspberries

TO FINISH
yellow food colouring paste
a few fresh raspberries

RASPBERRY & YUZU CAKE

If raspberry lemonade is your bag, then this cake might just be your brand new bag! The blend of familiar sweet raspberry with the other-worldly citrus flavour of yuzu (which is a bit like a combination of mandarin, grapefruit and lime) lifts this cake to zesty, practically effervescent heights. It is the perfect cake for a summer party.

———

Make your Raspberry Goo (page 60), Yuzu Curd (page 58), Yuzu Buttercream and Raspberry Buttercream (page 36), and set aside.

FOR THE RASPBERRY RIPPLE SPONGE

Preheat your oven to 190°C (170°C fan) and grease four 20cm/8in round sandwich tins.

In the bowl of a stand mixer fitted with the paddle attachment, or a large mixing bowl, beat together the sugar, butter and oil for 2-3 minutes until light and pale in colour. Add the eggs, two at a time, beating well after each addition for 30 seconds. Sift the flour directly into the bowl and fold it in, either by hand using a large metal spoon or on the lowest speed on the mixer. When there is only a bit of flour left to incorporate, add the milk and vanilla and continue to fold until everything is well combined.

Add 2-3 tablespoons of raspberry goo to the bowl, then use a rubber spatula to ripple it through the batter, without fully mixing it in. Scoop up that bit of rippled batter and pop it into one of the tins. Continue this process until you have used roughly half a batch of raspberry goo and all of your tins have the same amount of goo-rippled batter in them. Carefully level the tops with a palette knife without mixing the goo in too much.

Bake for 22-24 minutes until a skewer inserted into the middle of each sponge comes out clean.

Leave to cool for 15-20 minutes before removing from the tins and allowing the sponges to cool completely.

FOR THE WHITE CHOCOLATE DISCS

Line a baking sheet with greaseproof paper or a silpat.

Melt the white chocolate as described on page 19, then pour it onto the baking sheet and spread it out with a palette knife to about 2mm thick. While the chocolate is wet, sprinkle the freeze-dried raspberry bits over the top and leave to semi-set. This will happen quite quickly if the chocolate   >

Cakes

< is tempered; if not, just put it into the fridge for a couple of minutes. Use a small round cookie cutter to press circles into the chocolate, leaving it to set completely before removing them.

TO FINISH
Level and trim the sponges (see QR code on page 210) and use a cake leveller, or a long serrated bread knife, to split each layer through the middle so that you have 8 thin layers in total. Handle these carefully. Stick the first layer onto a cake board or a large, flat plate using a small amount of buttercream, then layer up your cake with alternating fillings of raspberry buttercream with raspberry goo and yuzu buttercream with yuzu curd (watch how to do this on the QR code on page 210). Place in the fridge for 10–20 minutes to firm up.

Neaten up the chilled cake by cutting any lumps and bumps off the edges with a serrated knife.

Crumb-coat the top and sides of the cake with the yuzu buttercream (see the QR code on page 210), then chill in the fridge for at least 30 minutes, or until firm to the touch.

Give the cake a smooth top coat using the yuzu buttercream and chill again until it is firm to the touch.

Meanwhile, colour the remaining yuzu buttercream with a little yellow food colouring paste and transfer to a large piping bag with a large petal piping nozzle.

To decorate your cake, apply blobs of raspberry buttercream and dot them over the sides and top of the cake, spreading them a bit with the cake scraper. Repeat, but this time use blobs of raspberry goo, dotted about randomly and spread out. Pipe lots of ruffley wiggles all over the top and sides of the cake with the yellow yuzu buttercream, then finish the cake with some white chocolate discs and fresh raspberries.

––––

TEAM TIP
Some supermarkets sell yuzu juice in their World Food sections, but you can also buy it online. Check that the ingredients are 100% yuzu juice, as sometimes it can be found as 'yuzu seasoning', which contains other ingredients.

Makes 1 x 20cm/8in
cake to serve 12-16

PREP
2 x batches of Honey
Swiss Meringue
Buttercream
(page 40)

PEANUT SPONGE
330g unsalted butter,
   softened
200g smooth peanut
   butter (we like Skippy)
135g vegetable oil
500g caster sugar
¼ tsp sea salt

8 eggs
500g self-raising flour
6 tbsp milk

PEANUT MALTY
CORNFLAKES
160g plain cornflakes
80g salted peanuts,
   finely chopped

40g malted milk
   powder (such
   as Horlicks)
40g caster sugar
¼ tsp sea salt
100g unsalted
   butter, melted
30g smooth
   peanut butter

HONEY CRUNCHY NUT CAKE

If you thought the Malty Cornflakes couldn't be improved, you were wrong. Adding peanut butter and salty chopped peanuts amps up their addictive credentials to eleven! This cake is really just an excuse to use as much of the stuff as possible. Peanut sponge, honey Swiss meringue buttercream and more peanutty, malty cornflakes than you can shake a stick at. The only trouble is it tastes too good!

——

Make the Honey Swiss Meringue Buttercream (page 40), cover and set aside.

FOR THE PEANUT SPONGE
Preheat your oven to 190°C (170°C fan) and grease four 20cm/8in round sandwich tins.

In a stand mixer fitted with the paddle attachment, or a large mixing bowl, beat together the butter, peanut butter, oil, sugar and salt on a medium speed until pale and fluffy. Add the eggs, two at a time, beating well after each addition. Sift in the flour and fold carefully through, either on the lowest speed on the mixer or by hand using a large metal spoon. Before the flour is fully mixed in, add the milk and continue to stir until you have a thick, smooth batter.

Divide the batter among the prepared tins and level the tops with a palette knife. Bake for 22-24 minutes until a skewer inserted into the centre of each sponge comes out clean.

Leave to cool for 15-20 minutes before removing from the tins and allowing to cool completely.

FOR THE PEANUT MALTY CORNFLAKES
Reduce the oven to 170°C (150°C fan). Line two baking trays with greaseproof paper.

In a large bowl, combine the cornflakes and chopped peanuts.

Whisk together the malt powder, sugar and salt in a separate small bowl and set aside.

In the microwave or a small pan over a low heat, melt the butter and peanut butter together and stir to combine, then pour the mixture all over the cornflakes and peanuts. Stir well to coat each flake in butter. Sprinkle over the dry ingredients and stir to ensure every bit of it is now covered in the mixture.

Spread the flakes out across the baking trays and bake for 10 minutes.   >

< Remove from the oven, give the flakes a little shuffle to separate them and leave to cool completely.

TO FINISH
Level and trim the sponges (see QR code on page 210) and stick the first layer of sponge onto a cake board or a large, flat plate using a little honey Swiss meringue buttercream. Smother that in a generous, even layer of the buttercream, then sprinkle some of the peanut malty cornflakes over the top.

Build up the next two layers in the same way, finishing off with the final sponge upside down for a neat top.

Use the honey buttercream to crumb-coat the top and sides of the cake (see QR code on page 210) and chill in the fridge for at least 30 minutes until firm to the touch.

Apply a top coat of buttercream to the chilled cake, smoothing out and removing the excess with a cake scraper.

Now you're going to cover the whole cake in peanut malty cornflakes! The best way to do this is to put your cake (and turntable, if you're using one) onto the largest tray you have (a roasting tray works well) to catch the fallen cornflakes. Grab the cornflakes by the handful and press them into the sides, starting at the bottom and working your way up to the top, covering the entire cake in flakes. If you have any large gaps you might want to poke individual flakes in there to achieve a more uniform look. Any leftover flakes, or those that fell into the roasting tray, for goodness' sake save those in an airtight container for emergency nibbles!

Makes 1 x 20cm/8in
cake to serve 12-16

PREP
1 x batch of Salted
Caramel Buttercream
(page 44)
1 x batch of Vanilla
Buttercream (page 36)

CHOCOLATE SPONGE
650g plain flour
690g caster sugar
120g cocoa powder
2 tsp bicarbonate of
soda
1 tsp sea salt
6 eggs
450g brewed or instant
coffee, cooled

450g buttermilk
390g vegetable oil

TO FINISH
½ jar of Lotus Biscoff
spread, warmed slightly
so that it's runny
½ packet of Lotus Biscoff
biscuits, mostly crushed
but 4-5 broken into small
pieces

20g dark chocolate,
melted and cooled
1 x batch of Dark
Chocolate Drip
Ganache (page 52)
1 x batch of Italian
Meringue (page 48)

S'MORES CAKE

This beast of a cake takes every delicious element of the celebrated American campfire classic and morphs them into cake form. With salted caramel buttercream between moist chocolate sponge, packed with biscuits and topped generously with torched Italian meringue, diving into this S'mores cake will give you all those fireside feels.

———

Make the Salted Caramel Buttercream (page 44) and the Vanilla Buttercream (page 36), cover and set aside for later.

FOR THE CHOCOLATE SPONGE
Preheat your oven to 190°C (170°C fan) and grease four 20cm/8in round sandwich tins.

In a medium bowl, whisk together the flour, sugar, cocoa, bicarb and salt.

In a separate large bowl (the largest you've got!), whisk together the remaining ingredients until combined.

Add the dry mixture to the wet mixture and whisk until you have a thick, runny, lump-free batter. Distribute the batter evenly among the prepared tins, then bake for 24–30 minutes, or until a skewer

inserted into the middle of each sponge comes out clean.

Leave to cool for 20 minutes before removing from the tins and leaving to cool completely.

TO FINISH
Level and trim your sponges (see QR code on page 210). Stick the first layer onto a cake board or a large, flat plate using some caramel buttercream. Layer up your sponges, filling each one with a generous spreading of buttercream, a drizzle of Biscoff spread and a sprinkling of biscuit crumbs (keep some of these back for the decoration). Finish with an upside-down sponge for the top layer.

Crumb-coat the top and sides of the cake with the vanilla buttercream (see QR code on page 210) and chill for 30 minutes, or until the icing is firm to the touch.

Give the chilled cake a top coat with vanilla buttercream, then put it in the fridge for 10 minutes to set. Meanwhile, take a small portion of the remaining buttercream and stir some melted cooled chocolate into it until it's completely combined. Using a palette knife, spread a band of this   >

<   around the bottom of the chilled cake, to about a third of the way up, then smooth it out with a cake scraper to create a band that sits a little proud of the top coat. Chill the cake again for 10 minutes.

Meanwhile, make the Drip Ganache as directed on page 52. While it is still runny, pour it into a small piping bag and add drips around the edge of the cake, spaced about 5cm/2in apart.

Put the remaining ganache into a small bowl and allow to set until it's a spreadable consistency, then use a palette knife to apply a band of it around the bottom of the cake, reaching halfway up the chocolate buttercream band. Chill for another 10 minutes, then finish this bottom section with a band of biscuit crumbs pressed carefully into the bottom half of the ganache.

Put the remaining slightly warm Biscoff spread into a piping bag and snip a little bit off the end. Use this to add drips that fall between the chocolate ganache drips that you did earlier.

Make your Italian Meringue (page 48), then dollop it in a big pile on top of the cake in a kind of orderly, considered mess! Use a kitchen blowtorch to carefully toast the meringue, being careful not to toast the ganache and the rest of the cake at the same time! Finish it all off by poking little pieces of Biscoff biscuits into the meringue.

Makes 1 x 20cm/8in
cake to serve 12–16

PREP
1 x batch of Swiss
  Meringue Buttercream
  (page 40)
1 x batch of Matcha
  Swiss Meringue
  Buttercream
  (page 40)

1 x batch of Matcha Pie
Crumb (page 64)

BLACK SESAME PASTE
30g black sesame seeds

MATCHA SPONGE
500g caster sugar
135g vegetable oil
330g unsalted butter,
  softened

8 eggs
500g self-raising flour
1½ tsp matcha green
  tea powder
6 tbsp milk
1 tsp vanilla extract

**CANDIED BLACK
SESAME SEEDS**
2 tbsp black sesame seeds,
  roasted for 5 minutes in
  the oven and cooled

1 tsp water
1 tbsp icing sugar, sifted

TO FINISH
100g white chocolate
2–4 tsp matcha green
  tea powder
1–2 tsp black sesame
  seeds

MATCHA & BLACK SESAME CAKE

Two of the most divisive ingredients
in one cake... Are we mad? No, we're
professionals, you can trust us. This cake
is a classy little number that takes the
unique and delicate matcha flavour and
teams it up with the nutty roastiness of
black sesame, combining them to create
an 8-layer tower of delicious, soft sponge,
decorated with an ombre-style blending
of both matcha and black sesame Swiss
meringue buttercreams.

———

Make your Swiss Meringue Buttercream
and Matcha Swiss Meringue Buttercream
(page 40) and Matcha Pie Crumb (page 64),
and set aside.

FOR THE BLACK SESAME PASTE
Gently toast the black sesame seeds in a
hot oven for 5 minutes. While still warm, tip
them into a food processor or spice grinder
and process until they turn into a runny paste
(this can take 15–20 minutes). If you don't
have an electric-powered assistant, you can
use a pestle and mortar, but you won't be
able to achieve the same consistency. Your
buttercream will still be delicious, just a bit
more speckly in appearance.

Stir the black sesame paste into the batch
of plain Swiss meringue buttercream until
thoroughly combined. Cover and set aside.

FOR THE MATCHA SPONGE
Preheat your oven to 190°C (170°C fan) and
grease four 20cm/8in round sandwich tins.

In a stand mixer fitted with the paddle
attachment, or a large mixing bowl, beat
together the sugar, oil and butter for a
couple of minutes until light and fluffy. Add
the eggs, two at a time, beating well after
each addition. Sift together the flour and
matcha powder and add to the mixture,
folding in carefully with a large metal spoon
or simply on the lowest setting on the
mixer. When almost all of the flour has been
incorporated, add the milk and vanilla and
continue to fold until you have a smooth,
thick batter.

Distribute the batter evenly among the
prepared tins and level the tops with a
palette knife. Bake for 22–24 minutes until
a skewer inserted into the centre of each
sponge comes out clean.   >

< Leave to cool for 15-20 minutes before removing from the tins and allowing to cool completely.

FOR THE CANDIED BLACK SESAME SEEDS

Line a small baking tray with greaseproof paper.

In a small bowl, mix together the roasted black sesame seeds, water and icing sugar, until all of the seeds are evenly coated. Spread the seeds over the baking tray and bake in the oven for 7-8 minutes, then leave to cool completely.

Once cool, break them up into tiny nuggets and set aside.

TO FINISH

Level and trim the sponges (see the QR code on page 210 for how it's done) and use a cake leveller, or a long serrated bread knife, to split each layer through the middle so that you have 8 thin, fragile layers in total. Stick the first layer of sponge onto a cake board or a large, flat plate using a little buttercream.

Cover the first sponge with a generous, even layer of the matcha buttercream. Place the next layer of sponge carefully on top of that and repeat, but this time with black sesame buttercream. Keep layering up the sponges, alternating the buttercreams and when you come to the final sponge, turn it upside down to get a nice smooth top. Chill the cake for 20 minutes, or until firm.

Neaten up the chilled cake by cutting any lumps and bumps off the edges with a serrated knife (see the QR code on page 210).

Use either buttercream to crumb-coat the top and sides of the cake (see page 210), then chill again for at least 30 minutes.

To achieve a blended look, start by applying a generous amount of black sesame buttercream to the bottom half of the cake. Before you smooth this out, apply a generous amount of the matcha buttercream to the top and upper section of the sides, to meet the black sesame buttercream beneath. Use your cake scraper to remove the excess and smooth the sides with the help of a turntable. As you do so, the two different buttercreams will blend together. Smooth the top of the cake with your cake scraper.

It's entirely up to you how you decorate this cake. We wanted ours to look like a fancy dessert from a posh restaurant so we melted some white chocolate to form into tiles and discs, which we sprinkled with black sesame seeds or painted with a little matcha powder mixed with water. We then melted some white chocolate mixed with matcha to make little balls in truffle moulds. Finally, we sprinkled the cake with some matcha pie crumb and the candied black sesame seeds. Go wild!

Makes 1 x 20cm/8in cake to serve 12-16

PREP
1 x batch of Smooth Hazelnut Butter (page 62)
1 x batch of Hazelnut Buttercream (page 36)
1 x batch of Meringue Poops (page 45)

CHOCOLATE SPONGE
325g plain flour
345g caster sugar
60g cocoa powder
1 tsp bicarbonate of soda
½ tsp sea salt
3 eggs
225g brewed or instant coffee, cooled
225g buttermilk
195g vegetable oil

HAZELNUT SPONGE
250g caster sugar
165g unsalted butter, softened
67g vegetable oil
a pinch of sea salt
4 eggs
250g self-raising flour
3 tbsp milk
50g Hazelnut Butter (see Prep)

TO FINISH
100g dark chocolate chips, for decorating the Meringue Poops
200g chopped, roasted hazelnuts
edible gold lustre
1 x batch of Buttery Ganache Icing (page 52)
½ jar of Nutella, warmed slightly
1 x batch of Dark Chocolate Drip Ganache (page 52)

FERRERO ROCHER CAKE

You want a project? You've got one! The Ferrero Rocher cake has 8 layers, multiple fillings, gold-splattered nutty meringues and even a ganache drip! It's the ultimate example of the importance of being prepared. Take your time and get everything ready so you can enjoy the process. You'll be the talk of the party when you rock up with this total showstopper!

———

Make the Hazelnut Butter (page 62), Hazelnut Buttercream (page 36) and Meringue Poops (page 45), and set aside.

FOR THE CHOCOLATE SPONGE
Preheat your oven to 190°C (170°C fan) and grease four 20cm/8in round sandwich tins.

In a mixing bowl, whisk together the flour, sugar, cocoa, bicarb and salt. In a separate bowl, whisk together the eggs, cooled coffee, buttermilk and oil until well combined. Add the dry ingredients to the bowl of wet ingredients and whisk to combine completely.

Divide the batter between two of the prepared tins and bake for 24-30 minutes, or until a skewer inserted into the middle of each sponge comes out clean.

Leave to cool for 15-20 minutes before removing from the tins and allowing to cool completely.

FOR THE HAZELNUT SPONGE
Meanwhile, in a stand mixer fitted with the paddle attachment, or a mixing bowl, beat the sugar, butter, oil and salt on a medium speed for a couple of minutes until pale and fluffy. Add the eggs, one at a time, and beat well after each addition. Sift the flour directly into the bowl and begin folding on the lowest speed of the stand mixer or using a large metal spoon or a spatula. When there is still some flour left to be incorporated, add the milk and hazelnut butter and fold gently to combine everything.

Divide the batter between the two remaining tins, levelling the tops with a palette knife. Bake for 22-24 minutes, or until an inserted skewer comes out clean.

Leave to cool for 15-20 minutes before removing from the tins and allowing to cool completely.   >

Cakes

236

<   **TO DECORATE THE MERINGUE POOPS**
Melt the chocolate chips using the method on page 19. Get a wide, shallow bowl of chopped hazelnuts ready. Line a baking sheet with a silpat or greaseproof paper.

Dip each meringue into the melted chocolate so that it reaches about a third of the way up the sides. Remove the chocolate from the bottoms by wiping it on the edge of the bowl. Cover the chocolate-covered sides of the poops in chopped hazelnuts. Try to avoid getting the nuts on the underside of the poops, so that they can be placed level on top of the cake. Leave to set on the baking sheet. Keep the remaining hazelnuts for decorating.

As an extra touch, spray or splatter the poops with some edible gold lustre.

TO FINISH
Start by making the Buttery Ganache Icing as directed on page 52, to give it time to set to a spreadable consistency.

Level and trim the sponges (see QR code on page 210) and use a cake leveller, or a long serrated bread knife, to split each layer through the middle so that you have 8 thin layers in total. These will be fragile so handle them very carefully. Stick a layer of chocolate sponge onto a cake board or a large, flat plate using a small blob of buttercream. Top with a generous even layer of the hazelnut buttercream and sprinkle all over with some of the chopped hazelnuts.

Next, place a layer of hazelnut sponge on top and apply a thick layer of hazelnut buttercream. Using a palette knife, remove some of the buttercream to create a shallow

divot in the middle, about 2.5cm/1in from the edge, then fill the gap with Nutella (warming it a little makes it easier to spread).

Repeat the two previous steps, alternating the sponges and the fillings as you build the cake up. To see how we do it, head to the QR codes on page 210. Finish with the final layer upside down for a neat top, then chill for 20 minutes.

Neaten up the chilled cake by cutting any lumps and bumps off the edges with a serrated knife. Use the buttery ganache to crumb-coat the trimmed cake (see page 210), then chill the cake again for at least 30 minutes, or until the ganache has set.

Give the chilled cake a final top coat of the buttery ganache, and use a palette knife to add some texture to the sides. Using your hands, scoop up the remaining chopped hazelnuts and gently press them into the sides around the bottom half of the cake to create a band of nutty nibs.

Make the Chocolate Drip Ganache (page 52) and transfer to a piping bag. Pipe a drip around the edges (see page 210). Fill in the middle with the remaining ganache and spread it over the top of the cake with a palette knife. Chill for 15 minutes until set.

Put the remaining buttercream into a large piping bag fitted with a star-shaped nozzle and pipe rosettes all around the top of the cake, about 1cm/½in apart.

Place the jazzy meringue poops on top of each rosette, pressing down a little, to complete the cake!

Cakes

Makes 1 x 20cm/8in
cake to serve 12-16

PREP
2 x batches of Swiss
  Meringue Buttercream
  (page 40)
1 x batch of Crème
  Pâtissière (page 50)

STICKY TOFFEE SPONGE
450g pitted, soft dates
  (such as Medjool)
6 balls of stem ginger,
  chopped
525g boiling water
3 tsp bicarbonate of soda
225g unsalted butter,
  softened

450g soft light brown
  sugar
6 eggs
525g self-raising flour
1½ tsp ground ginger
1½ tsp ground
  cinnamon
½ tsp ground nutmeg
¾ tsp sea salt

STICKY TOFFEE SAUCE
160g unsalted butter
160g dark muscavado
  sugar
200g double cream
½ tsp Marmite
a pinch of sea salt

STICKY TOFFEE CAKE

When you work at Crumbs & Doilies it's tradition that you receive a cake on your birthday and, more often than not, they are off-menu, one-of-a-kind cakes that the bakery team magics up from their wild imaginations! This recipe is based on one that Rosie made for Hannah, whose favourite dessert is Sticky Toffee Pudding (she's not the only one). In my opinion, the classic pud has to be served with custard, so naturally we have filled this cake with pools of crème pât as well as oozy sticky toffee sauce.

————

Make the Swiss Meringue Buttercream (page 40) and the Crème Pâtissière (page 50), cover and set aside.

FOR THE STICKY TOFFEE SPONGE
Preheat your oven to 190°C (170°C fan) and grease four 20cm/8in round sandwich tins.

In a small bowl, combine the dates, stem ginger, boiling water and bicarb and set aside for 5 minutes before blitzing to a purée in a food processor.

In a stand mixer fitted with the paddle attachment, or a large mixing bowl, beat the butter and sugar together until pale and fluffy. Add the eggs, one at a time, beating well for 30 seconds after each addition. Meanwhile, sift the flour, spices and salt together. When the eggs are all incorporated, add the dry ingredients and fold them through gently, either on the lowest speed on the mixer or by hand using a large metal spoon. When the dry ingredients have almost been incorporated, add the date purée and continue to fold the mixture slowly until you have a smooth, thick batter.

Divide the batter among the prepared tins and bake for 22-24 minutes, or until a skewer inserted into the centre of each sponge comes out clean.

Leave to cool for 15-20 minutes before removing from the tins and allowing to cool completely.

FOR THE STICKY TOFFEE SAUCE
Combine the butter, sugar and cream in a small saucepan and heat gently over a low heat, stirring constantly until all of the sugar has completely dissolved.

Remove from the heat and stir in the Marmite and salt. Leave to cool completely.   >

< TO FINISH

Preheat your oven to 150°C (130°C fan) and line a baking tray with greaseproof paper.

Take your Swiss meringue buttercream and mix in half of the sticky toffee sauce, then cover and set aside.

Fill a piping bag with the crème pâtissière.

Level and trim the sponges (see the QR code on page 210). Hang on to those trimmings - we have a plan for those! Stick the first sponge onto a cake board or a large, flat plate usinga little buttercream.

Smooth a generous dollop of the sticky toffee buttercream all over this layer, then use a small offset palette knife to scrape a shallow divot out of the centre, about 2.5cm/1in from the edge of the cake. Inside this, pipe a thick ring of crème pât, then fill the space inside that with some sticky toffee sauce. Level it out a little with a palette knife before topping with the next layer of sponge.

Repeat the above process with the next two layers and top the cake by turning the final layer of sponge upside down.

Give the top and sides a crumb-coat of sticky toffee buttercream (see the QR code on page 210) and put into the fridge to set for at least 30 minutes.

Meanwhile, grab those cake trimmings. Crumble the best bits up into chunky crumbs and scatter all over the prepared baking tray, then bake for 45 minutes- 1 hour until they are dried out and crunchy. Leave to cool.

Give the chilled cake a final top coat with the buttercream and get it as smooth as possible with a cake smoother or palette knife. Put the cake back in the fridge for about 10 minutes to firm up.

Using a small palette knife, apply small blobs of sticky toffee sauce to the sides of the chilled cake, then use a cake smoother or palette knife to create a swipe effect.

Put the remaining sticky toffee buttercream into a piping bag fitted with a star nozzle and pipe little rosettes all around the top of the cake right next to each other. Flood the middle with the remaining sticky toffee sauce, spreading it out with the back of a spoon if you need to. Top the ring of rosettes with chunks of the crunchy cake crumbs to finish.

Makes 1 x 20cm/8in
cake to serve 12-16

PREP
2 x batches of
Lemon Buttercream
(page 36)

2 x batches of Lemon
Curd (page 58)
1 x batch of Plain Pie
Crumb (page 64)
1 x batch of messy
French Meringues
(page 45)

LEMON SPONGE
500g caster sugar
330g unsalted
butter, softened
135g vegetable oil
zest of 8 unwaxed
lemons

8 eggs
500g self-raising flour
3 tbsp freshly
squeezed
lemon juice
3 tbsp milk

LEMON MESS CAKE

A mash up of two classic British desserts: Eton mess and lemon drizzle cake, both of which are simple but irresistible, with their respective crispy creaminess and zingy zestiness! On the menu for over a decade, this truly unique cake does justice to both, using fluffy lemon sponges filled with creamy lemon buttercream, tart lemon curd, crunchy pie crumb and an absurd amount of meringue.

───

Make your Lemon Buttercream (page 36), Lemon Curd (page 58), Plain Pie Crumb (page 64) and French Meringues (page 45) and set aside.

FOR THE LEMON SPONGE
Preheat your oven to 190°C (170°C fan) and grease four 20cm/8in round sandwich tins.

In the bowl of a stand mixer fitted with the paddle attachment, or a large mixing bowl, beat together the sugar, butter, oil and lemon zest for a couple of minutes until pale and fluffy. Add the eggs, two at a time, beating for 30 seconds in between each addition. Sift the flour directly over the mixture and fold it through gently either at the lowest speed or with a large metal spoon. Once almost all of the flour has been incorporated, add the lemon juice and milk, and continue to fold the mixture until you have a light, smooth batter.

Distribute the batter evenly among the four tins and spread it out with a palette knife to even the tops. Bake for 22-24 minutes, or until a skewer inserted into the centre of each sponge comes out clean.

Leave to cool for 15-20 minutes before removing from the tins and allowing to cool completely.

TO FINISH
Level and trim your sponges (see the QR code on page 210), then stick the first layer onto a cake board or a large, flat plate using a little bit of lemon buttercream.

Using an offset palette knife, spread a generous, even layer of lemon buttercream all over the sponge. Using the palette knife, remove some of the buttercream from the middle, 2-3cm/1in from the edge of the cake, to create a shallow divot. Spoon a couple of tablespoons of lemon curd into the divot and spread out (see how we do this by using the QR code on page 210), then sprinkle the whole thing with some pie crumb. Repeat for the next two layers.   >

<   Finish with the final layer of sponge upside down for a neat top.

Crumb-coat the top and sides of the cake with the buttercream (see the QR code on page 210), then chill in the fridge for at least 30 minutes, or until firm to the touch.

Remove the cake from the fridge and give it a generous top coat with lemon buttercream, removing the excess as you smooth out the sides and top with a cake scraper or palette knife. Chill for another 10 minutes or so.

Take some lemon curd on a small palette knife and, keeping it parallel to the cake, sweep it around the sides to create yellow lemon curd swipes all over the surface of the cake. Put the rest of the curd in a small piping bag and pipe some drips around the top edge of the cake.

Break up the meringues into pieces and mix roughly two-thirds of them into the remaining lemon buttercream. Pile the meringue buttercream on the top of the cake in the middle, then finish with the last of the meringue pieces, a lemon curd drizzle and a scattering of pie crumb.

———

TEAM TIP
Filling cake with lemon curd can make the layers slide all over the place when you're decorating. If this happens to you, just chill the cake for 10 minutes before adding the crumb-coat.

Makes 1 x 20cm/8in
cake to serve 12-16

PREP
2 x batches of Salted
  Caramel Buttercream
  (page 44)

1 x batch of Salted
  Caramel (page 42)

SYRUP SPONGE
240g unsalted butter
240g soft dark brown sugar

480g golden syrup
½ tsp sea salt
115g eggs (3 small)
320g milk
480g self-raising flour

SALTY SHARDS
55g caster sugar
1 tbsp water
10g unsalted butter
a pinch of flaky sea salt,
  plus extra to decorate

SALTED CARAMEL CAKE

While caramel is incredibly versatile, can be used in a myriad of ways and appears all over this book in some of our most excting and iconic bakes, sometimes it just needs a chance to shine and be the hero. This cake is unashamedly caramel-y! The syrup sponge is out-of-this-world moist and is the perfect vessel for lifting up and showing off the king of the sugary stuff.

———

Make the Salted Caramel Buttercream (page 44) and Salted Caramel (page 42), then leave to cool, cover and set aside.

FOR THE SYRUP SPONGE
eheat your oven to 190°C (170°C fan) a gi ease four 20cm/8in round sandwich tin

In a medium saucepan, melt the butter with the su ar, golden syrup and salt over a low heat, stirring until the sugar has dissolved completely. Remove from the heat and allow to cool.

Meanwhile, in a large mixing bowl, whisk together the eggs and milk until thoroughly combined. Pour in the cooled sugar mixture and whisk together. Sift the flour directly into the bowl and whisk until you have a smooth, lump-free batter.

Distribute the batter evenly among the four tins and bake for 23-25 minutes, or until a skewer inserted into the centre of each sponge comes out clean.

Cool for 15-20 minutes, then remove from the tins and allow to cool completely.

FOR THE SALTY SHARDS
Line a baking sheet with a silpat or greaseproof paper.

Put the sugar and water into a small saucepan and stir it briefly to ensure the sugar is soaked evenly. Set it over a medium heat and without stirring, allow it to bubble away When the mixture is a rich u r oui, remove from the heat and n ne butter until it has melted completely.

Pour the mixture onto the prepared baking sheet, allowing it to spread out on its own. Leave for a minute before sprinkling the flaky sea salt all over the top. Allow to cool completely before breaking up into shards.

TO FINISH
Level and trim your sponges (see the QR code on page 210). Stick the first layer onto a cake board or a large, flat plate using a little bit of buttercream.   >

<   Spread a generous, even layer of salted caramel buttercream all over the sponge with a small offset palette knife. Then, with the palette knife set about 2.5cm/1in in from the outside edge, scrape off some of the buttercream to create a shallow divot (it should look like a side plate). Pour a couple of tablespoons of the salted caramel into the hollow and level it out with a palette knife (see how we do this by using the QR code on page 210).

Repeat the above step for the next two layers. Finish with the final layer of sponge upside down for a neat top.

Crumb-coat the top and sides of the cake with the buttercream (see the QR code on page 210), then chill in the fridge for at least 30 minutes.

Once the icing is firm to the touch, remove from the fridge and give it a generous top coat of the salted caramel buttercream, removing the excess as you smooth out the sides and top with a cake scraper or palette knife.

Finish the cake with a salted caramel drip around the edge (see page 210), then flood the top with more caramel to fill the space on the top of the cake.

Take a spoonful of the leftover salted caramel and draw a line of it up the inside of a large piping bag fitted with a round nozzle, then fill the piping bag with the remaining salted caramel buttercream. Pipe little caramel swirled blobs around the top of the cake and finish by poking pieces of salty shards into each blob. Give the top of the cake a final sprinkling of flaky sea salt.

Makes 1 x 20cm/8in
cake to serve 12–16

PREP
1 x batch of Raspberry
  Goo (page 60)

**VEGAN CHOCOLATE
SPONGE**
575g soya milk
2½ tsp cider vinegar
515g self-raising flour
70g cocoa powder

1 tsp bicarbonate
  of soda
4 tsp baking powder
¼ tsp sea salt
480g caster sugar
290g vegan butter
  alternative, softened
1 tsp vanilla extract

**VEGAN RASPBERRY
BUTTERCREAM**
570g vegan butter
  alternative, softened

900g icing sugar, sifted
2–4 tbsp Raspberry Goo
  (see Prep)
1 tbsp soya or other milk
  alternative, to loosen
¼ tsp sea salt

VEGAN GANACHE DRIP
80g dark chocolate
  chips (check to ensure
  it's vegan)
80g vegan butter
  alternative

TO FINISH
100g pistachios,
  chopped
a little melted dark
  chocolate (optional)
a little Pistachio
  Butter (page 62)
  (optional)
pink food colouring
  (optional)
10g freeze-dried
  raspberries

RASPBERRY, PISTACHIO & CHOCOLATE CAKE

This is a cake that will please everyone, regardless of whether they are vegan or not, thanks to the winning combo of raspberry, chocolate and pistachio flavours. This plant-based beauty will convince all the doubters out there that vegan bakes can not only taste exceptional, they can look incredible as well.

———

Prepare the Raspberry Goo as directed on page 60 and set aside

FOR THE VEGAN CHOCOLATE SPONGE
Preheat your oven to 190°C (170°C fan) and grease four 20cm/8in round sandwich tins.

In a small bowl, whisk together the soya milk and vinegar and allow to thicken for 5 minutes.

In another bowl, sift together the flour, cocoa, bicarb, baking powder and salt, and give it a whisk to combine.

In the bowl of a stand mixer fitted with the paddle attachment, or a large mixing

bowl, beat together the sugar, vegan butter alternative and vanilla until pale and fluffy, then add half of the dry ingredients and fold together. Pour in half of the thickened soya milk mixture and mix slowly. Repeat with the remaining dry ingredients and soya mixture until thoroughly combined, making sure you give the sides and bottom of the bowl a good scrape to ensure it's all mixed in and you have a thick, lump-free batter.

Distribute the batter evenly among the prepared tins and level the tops with a palette knife. Bake for 22–24 minutes until a skewer inserted into the centre of each sponge comes out clean.

Leave to cool for 15–20 minutes before removing from the tins and allowing to cool completely.

**FOR THE VEGAN RASPBERRY
BUTTERCREAM**
In a stand mixer fitted with the paddle attachment, or a large bowl, beat your vegan butter alternative for 5 minutes on a high speed until light and whippy. Add the   >

< icing sugar in two stages, beating for 3–5 minutes after each addition. Before you add the raspberry goo, take out 2 large spoonfuls of icing and keep until later on. Add the goo to the remaining icing and beat for 2 minutes. If it feels too stiff, add 1–2 tablespoons of milk alternative to loosen. You should end up with a fluffy, smooth, spreadable buttercream.

TO FINISH

Level the tops of each sponge (see the QR code on page 210), but don't trim the edges. This sponge can be a little crumbly and keeping the edges on will make it much easier to crumb-coat. Stick the first layer of sponge onto a cake board or a large, flat plate using a little blob of buttercream. Spread with a generous layer of raspberry buttercream, raspberry goo and a sprinkling of chopped pistachio nuts.

Build up the layers as above, finishing with the final sponge upside down on top for a neat finish.

Crumb-coat the whole cake with the raspberry buttercream (see the QR code on page 210) and chill for at least 30 minutes, or until firm, before giving the chilled cake a smooth raspberry buttercream top coat (see page 210).

Make the vegan ganache drip by melting the chocolate and vegan butter alternative together in a microwave or over a bain-marie. Leave it to thicken slightly as it is much thinner than regular ganache.

Put the ganache drip into a piping bag and drip your cake as shown in the QR code on page 210. Return the cake to the fridge to set for 10 minutes.

Grab the buttercream that you saved earlier, split it in two, and add the melted dark chocolate to one half and pistachio butter to the other. Put all of the buttercreams, including any leftover raspberry buttercream (which you can colour with some pink food colouring if you wish), into multiple piping bags fitted with a variety of nozzles. Pipe swirls, blobs, ribbons and anything you fancy all over the top and across the bottom half of the cake to create a lush, textural decoration. Finish by sprinkling some more chopped pistachios and freeze-dried raspberries all over.

Cakes

Makes 1 x 20cm/8in cake to serve 12-16

PREP
1 x batch of Peanut
 Buttercream (page 36)
1 x batch of Salted
 Caramel (page 42)

CHOCOLATE SPONGE
325g plain flour
345g caster sugar
60g cocoa powder
1 tsp bicarbonate
 of soda
½ tsp sea salt
3 eggs
225g brewed or instant
 coffee, cooled
225g buttermilk
195g vegetable oil

PEANUT SPONGE
165g unsalted
 butter, softened
100g smooth peanut
 butter (we like Skippy)
250g caster sugar
67g vegetable oil
a pinch of sea salt
4 eggs
250g self-raising flour
3 tbsp milk

PEANUTTY NOUGAT
10g unsalted butter
35g caster sugar
10g evaporated milk
35g Marshmallow Fluff
⅛ tsp vanilla extract
10g peanut butter
25g salted peanuts,
 roughly chopped

TO FINISH
1 x batch of Buttery
 Ganache Icing
 (page 52)
a handful of salted
 peanuts, chopped

MARATHON CAKE

Arguably the king of chocolate bars, this cake is a tribute to the chocolate-covered, chewy, nutty, nougat-based treat we now know as Snickers. With eight layers of alternating peanut and chocolate sponges, filled with peanut buttercream, salted caramel and soft, chewy nougat, covered in a rich chocolate ganache, this is a project cake that will have people drooling.

———

Prepare the Peanut Buttercream (page 36) and Salted Caramel (page 42) and set aside.

Preheat your oven to 190°C (170°C fan) and grease four 20cm/8in round sandwich tins.

FOR THE CHOCOLATE SPONGE
Whisk together the flour, sugar, cocoa, bicarb and salt in a medium bowl.

In a separate large bowl, whisk together the eggs, coffee, buttermilk and oil, then add the dry ingredients to the wet and whisk thoroughly to combine until you have a smooth, runny batter.

Distribute the batter evenly between two of the tins and bake for 24-30 minutes until a skewer inserted into the centre of each sponge comes out clean. Leave to cool for 15-20 minutes before removing them from the tins.

FOR THE PEANUT SPONGE
Meanwhile, in the bowl of a stand mixer fitted with the paddle attachment, or a large mixing bowl, beat together the butter, peanut butter, sugar, oil and salt for a couple of minutes until pale and fluffy. Add the eggs, one at a time, beating well after each addition for about 30 seconds. Sift the flour directly into the bowl and fold it through the mixture on the slowest speed or using a large metal spoon. When the flour is almost all combined, add the milk and continue to slowly mix until thoroughly combined.

Divide the batter between the two remaining tins and level the tops with a palette knife. Bake for 22-24 minutes until a skewer inserted into the centre of each sponge comes out clean.

Leave to cool for 15-20 minutes before removing from the tins and allowing them to cool completely. >

< FOR THE PEANUTTY NOUGAT

In a small saucepan over a low-medium heat, melt the butter completely. Add the sugar and evaporated milk and heat, stirring constantly, until every grain of sugar has dissolved.

Remove from the heat and, while the mixture is still hot, add the Marshmallow Fluff, vanilla, peanut butter and chopped peanuts. Give it a good stir until thoroughly combined.

Pour into a heatproof bowl, cover and set aside to cool completely.

TO FINISH

Level and trim the sponges (see the QR code on page 210) and use a cake leveller, or a long serrated bread knife, to split each layer through the middle so that you have 8 thin layers in total. These will be pretty fragile so handle them very carefully. Stick the first layer of chocolate sponge onto a cake board or a large, flat plate using a small amount of buttercream.

Begin to build up your cake by alternating the sponge flavours and topping them with a generous layer of peanut buttercream, before adding alternate extra fillings of peanut nougat and salted caramel (see the QR code on page 210).

Give the whole cake a crumb-coat with peanut buttercream (see the QR code on page 210) and put it into the fridge to set for at least 30 minutes.

While your cake is chilling, make the Buttery Ganache Icing as directed on page 52, so that it has time to set to a spreadable consistency.

To decorate the cake with a 'fault line', like we do, start by applying a thick band of peanut buttercream all around the middle of the cake. Smooth it out carefully with a cake scraper. Chill for 10 minutes.

Next, apply a thin band of salted caramel over the top half of the previous buttercream band. Chill for a further 10 minutes.

Apply a thick band of buttery ganache all around the bottom section of the cake, only just overlapping the bottom of the peanut buttercream band. Smooth this out, but not too much, as you want the ganache to sit a little proud of the rest of the decoration. Repeat on the top section of the cake, overlapping the salted caramel section a tiny bit and smoothing out with the cake scraper.

Apply a generous amount of ganache to the top of the cake and smooth it out, then use the tip of the palette knife to wiggle some texture into it. Finish the cake by carefully studding the fault line with the chopped peanuts to resemble the chocolate bar!

1 x batch of Blueberry
  Buttercream (page 36)
1 x batch of Cream
  Cheese Icing (page 38)
1 x batch of Plain Pie
  Crumb (page 64)

LEMON SPONGE
330g unsalted butter,
  softened
135g vegetable oil
500g caster sugar
zest of 8 unwaxed lemons

8 eggs
500g self-raising flour
3 tbsp freshly squeezed
  lemon juice
3 tbsp milk

BLUEBERRY CHEESECAKE

Cakes

This cake has everything a good cheesecake should have and more! Zesty lemon sponge filled with tangy cream cheese icing, crunchy nuggets of pie crumb and sweet, deep purple blueberry goo, which transforms the buttercream to a beautiful, all-natural, purply pink colour. It's one of Sally's favourites as she goes nuts for a cheesecake in any form.

———

Make the Blueberry Goo (page 60), Blueberry Buttercream (page 36), Cream Cheese Icing (page 38) and Plain Pie Crumb (page 64), and set aside.

FOR THE LEMON SPONGE

Preheat your oven to 190°C (170°C fan) and grease four 20cm/8in round sandwich tins.

In the bowl of a stand mixer fitted with the paddle attachment, or a large mixing bowl, beat together the butter, oil, sugar and lemon zest for a couple of minutes until light and fluffy. Add the eggs, two at a time, beating for 30 seconds after each addition to make sure they're well incorporated, then sift in the flour. Start folding it through the mixture using a

large metal spoon or the lowest speed on the mixer. When the flour is almost all incorporated, add the lemon juice and milk and continue to fold the mixture until you have a smooth, thick batter.

Distribute the mixture evenly among the prepared tins, levelling the tops with a palette knife or the back of a spoon. Bake for 22-24 minutes, or until a skewer inserted into the centre of each sponge comes out clean.

Leave to cool for 15-20 minutes before removing from the tins and allowing them to cool completely.

TO FINISH

Level and trim your sponges (see the QR code on page 210) and use a cake leveller or a sharp, serrated bread knife to carefully split each sponge into two layers, so that you end up with 8 thin layers. Handle these very carefully as they will now be pretty fragile.

Stick the first layer of sponge onto a cake board or a large, flat plate using a bit of buttercream. Use an offset palette knife to spread a thick, even layer of cream cheese icing all over the sponge, then sprinkle   >

< some pie crumb over the top (make sure you keep some back for the decoration). Follow this with another layer of sponge, then spread with a thin layer of blueberry goo.

Repeat the above steps, building the cake with alternate layers of cream cheese icing and pie crumb, followed by blueberry goo. Keep the leftover cream cheese icing for the final decoration.

While the fillings are still soft, check how straight the cake is and push the sides here and there to correct any wonkiness. Chill in the fridge for 20 minutes.

Remove from the fridge and use a sharp serrated knife to trim down the sides of the cake to neaten it up if there are any wonky or lumpy sections.

Crumb-coat the top and sides of the cake with the blueberry buttercream (see the QR code on page 210), then chill in the fridge for at least 30 minutes, or until the icing is firm to the touch.

Remove the cake from the fridge and give it a tidy top coat (see the QR code on page 210) with the blueberry buttercream, smoothing out the sides and top with a cake scraper or a palette knife. Keep a little buttercream back for the final decoration.

Using a small palette knife, dot some little blobs of blueberry goo all around the sides of the cake, then use a cake scraper to spread them out horizontally, with the help of a turntable, so that you end up with a blueberry wash all over the sides. Try to spread rather than scrape so you don't remove any of the buttercream.

Put the last of the blueberry buttercream and cream cheese icing into piping bags with different nozzles and pipe a ring of cream cheese blobs around the edge of the top of the cake, and a ring of blueberry blobs inside of that. In between the two, sprinkle the remaining pie crumb.

Finish by pouring the remaining blueberry goo into the centre on top of the cake and carefully spread it to the edge of the piped buttercream to create a pool of goo.

Makes 1 x 20cm/8in
cake to serve 12-16

PREP
2 x batches of Burnt
  Butter (page 56)
1 x batch of Cookie
  Dough (page 66),
  frozen

2 x batches of Vanilla
  Buttercream (page 36)

**COOKIE DOUGH
SPONGE**
400g Burnt Butter (see
  Prep), at spreadable
  consistency
100g vegetable oil

375g caster sugar
125g soft dark
  brown sugar
8 eggs
500g self-raising flour
100g dark chocolate
  chips (50% cocoa
  solids)
6 tbsp milk

TO FINISH
120g dark chocolate
  chips, chopped
1 x batch of Dark Chocolate
  Drip Ganache (page 52)

COOKIE DOUGH CAKE

Cookie dough is one of our favourite ingredients in the bakery and we've made it the star of this 4-layer burnt butter, brown sugar cake. It's another C&D classic that's been around for years, with only a little tweak here and there, because he's just so perfect.

––––

Prepare the Burnt Butter (page 56) and the Cookie Dough (page 66) and set aside.

FOR THE COOKIE DOUGH SPONGE
Preheat your oven to 190°C (170°C fan) and grease and line the bottoms of four 20cm/8in round sandwich tins with greaseproof paper (see Tip).

In the bowl of a stand mixer fitted with the paddle attachment, or a large mixing bowl, beat together the burnt butter, oil and sugars on a medium speed for a couple of minutes until pale and fluffy. Add the eggs, two at a time, beating for 30 seconds after each addition to ensure they are well incorporated. Sift the flour directly into the mixture and fold it through either at the lowest speed or with a large metal spoon. Once you've got some of the flour integrated, add the chocolate chips and fold those in as well. Finally, with a few bits

of flour still remaining, add the milk and fold in until the batter is lovely and smooth (apart from the chocolate chips, of course!).

Distribute the batter evenly among the prepared tins and level the tops with a palette knife. Chop your frozen cookie dough into 1–2cm/½–¾in cubes and use a third of them to push into the batter across all four tins (return the remaining chunks to the freezer for later).

Bake for 22–24 minutes, or until a skewer inserted into the centre of the sponges comes out clean (try to poke a bit of cake, rather than cookie dough).

Leave to cool for 15–20 minutes before removing from the tins and carefully removing the greaseproof paper. Leave to cool completely.

TO FINISH
Level and trim your sponges (see the QR code on page 210). Stick the first layer onto a cake board or a large, flat plate using a little bit of the vanilla buttercream. Build up the cake layers with a generous, even amount of buttercream, a sprinkling of chocolate chips and a few chunks of the frozen cookie dough (roughly a third in total) in between each   >

< layer of sponge. Finish with the final layer upside down for a neat top.

Crumb-coat the top and sides of the cake with the buttercream (see the QR code on page 210), then chill in the fridge for at least 30 minutes, or until firm to the touch.

Remove the cake from the fridge and give it a generous top coat of vanilla buttercream, removing the excess as you smooth out the sides and top with a cake scraper or palette knife.

While the buttercream is still tacky, press the remaining chocolate chips around the bottom of the cake in a thick band, and then place some of the remaining chunks of cookie dough in and around the chocolate chips. Just make sure you keep a few back to decorate the top of the cake.

Prepare your Dark Chocolate Drip Ganache as directed on page 52 and transfer to a piping bag. Pipe zigzags of ganache across the top of the whole cake, then another set of zigzags crossing those, allowing it to drip down the sides when you reach the corners.

Put the remaining buttercream into a piping bag fitted with a star nozzle and pipe ruffles on top all around the edge of the cake. Push a cube of the remaining frozen cookie dough into the top of each one to finish.

———

TEAM TIP

Lining the bottoms of your cake tins with greaseproof paper will prevent the cookie dough pieces from sticking to the tins and make removing the sponge a whole lot easier.

Makes about 16

200g cake offcuts
50g Basic Buttercream
  (page 36) or Cream
  Cheese Icing (page 38)
250g chocolate of
  your choice

decorations of choice,
  such as sprinkles, pie
  crumb, freeze-dried
  fruit crumbs, etc.

CAKE BALLS

Cake pops, cake truffles, cake balls. Call them what you will, they are a fab way to use up your leftovers from trimming and levelling your cakes. Use different buttercreams and cake scraps to invent new flavours, cover them in chocolate and top them with sprinkles, pie crumb, malty cornflakes or even spray them gold.

You should use a 4:1 ratio of cake scraps to buttercream and this recipe is just an example. If you want to make more, or less, go nuts!

——

Line a tray with greaseproof paper or get a truffle mould ready.

In a mixing bowl, crumble up the cake offcuts between your fingers to a fine crumb. Add the buttercream or cream cheese icing a dollop at a time, mixing it through the crumbs until you have a consistency that will hold together tightly when squeezed.

Use your scales to weigh out 15g nuggets of the mixture and roll them into tidy little balls with your hands. Place them on the lined tray. If you are using a truffle mould, just pack the holes with the crumbs. Either way, put the cakey balls into the freezer to set for at least 1 hour.

When you're ready to decorate them, prepare a baking sheet with a silpat or greaseproof paper.

Melt your chocolate using the method on page 19 and put it into a small bowl, then dunk the balls carefully into the chocolate, turning them around in the bowl with a teaspoon until completely coated. Use a fork to remove each ball from the chocolate, allowing the excess to dribble back into the bowl, then carefully place on the baking sheet and decorate with your choice of sprinkle. If you have tempered the chocolate, it will begin to set pretty quickly so sprinkle any decorations on top as you go.

Cakes

ACKNOWLEDGEMENTS

Dear reader,

Thank you for picking up this book and being motivated to buy it. Whether you're a long-time fan of the Cupcake Jemma channel, a customer of Crumbs & Doilies, or you simply liked the look of the book and fancied having it on your shelf, I am grateful. But I need you to know something: I haven't written this book on my own. My name might be on the front but I would absolutely not have been able to write it if it wasn't for my amazing Crumbs & Doilies and Cupcake Jemma family, as well as the Michael Joseph team. Please join me in thanking them...

Thank you to the team at HQ, in particular Rosie, who single-handedly baked, filled and crumb-coated all the layer cakes in this book. And the team at C&D Soho, who put up with the inconvenience of the photoshoots with great patience.

To Nikki and Dane, who ran around baking, testing, re-testing, triple-re-testing, dancing, singing, photographing and filming the entire process, picking up so many forgotten ingredients from the supermarket and a million things in between. Thank you both so much.

Thank you to my work-wife-for-life, Sally. You quite literally helped me write this book, picked up on all the mistakes, organised everyone (including me), built multiple spreadsheets to keep the whole project on track, kept me sane through the process, kept me company on our commute and generally made the experience the most fun I've ever had at work! I am so grateful to have you as a friend and colleague (no YOU'RE crying!).

A massive thank you to my friend and business partner, Sam, whose meticulous eye, unwavering belief that things can always be better and dedication to Crumbs & Doilies helped us produce the perfect book. Sometimes I resist your help and advice because my ego takes it personally but since the very beginning all you've ever wanted to do was make Crumbs & Doilies the best it can possibly be, and me with it! So, thank you and sorry I resist so often.

And, of course, a huge thank you to the entire Michael Joseph team who have been on this journey with us: Dan, I'm so glad you slipped into my DMs and I'm honoured that you chose the Crumbs & Doilies book to be the first that you took on for MJ. I hope we did you proud! Emily, thank you for tweaking, pruning and polishing all of my writing and massive apologies for all the gazillion edits we sent every time you thought you'd finished! Chloe and Daisy, photographer-stylist combo extraordinaire! You understood the brief, big time! Watching the two of you work together was such a joy, truly inspiring and we had such a blast working with you to produce the beautiful pictures in this book. Lucy, the design of this book is perfect and makes us look as cool as we believe we are! Del, thank you too for stepping in to take the extra photos of the team and for making everyone feel so at ease.

Lastly, I want to thank my incredible husband and daughter. Kane, you put your life on hold so that I could work on this book. You dropped everything to look after Eden when I needed to travel to London every day for months to work. You never grumbled, even though it's been hard on us all. You've enabled me to connect with my work in a way I never have before so that I can produce something I am so proud of. And Eden, you have no idea how much coming home and squeezing you tight after a long day of baking, writing and shooting fills me up. I hope you grow up to be proud of your mummy. You will always be the best thing I've ever made.

Happy baking,

Love Jemma

INDEX

A

almonds: granola
    topping 104–6
apple corers 14
apples: apple crisps
    98–100
    apple crumble NY
        cookies 192
    apple pie cupcakes
        98–100
    apple sauce filling
        98–100
blackberry apple crumble
    cupcakes 104–6
caramel apple
    cheesecake 146

B

bain-maries 13
baking powder 17
baking sheets and trays 13
baklava cupcakes 86
bananas: banana
    blondie 142
    banana caramel 122–4
    bananarama
        cupcakes 122–4
berries: goo 60
    see also raspberries,
        strawberries etc
beurre noisette 56
bicarbonate of soda 17
birthday cake 212–14
birthday cake crumb 64
birthday cake NY
    cookies 180, 184
Biscoff spread: Biscoff
    buttercream 36, 194
Biscoff cookie cups 205–6
Biscoff rocky road 136
ginger & Biscoff NY
    cookies 188
s'mores cake 230–2
Swiss meringue
    buttercream 40
vegan Biscoff sandwich
    cookies 194
biscuits: cookie
    cheesecake 140
    OG cornflake crunch 148

s'mores brownie 157–8
    see also cookies;
        shortbread
Black Forest cupcakes
    125–6
black ganache 92–4
black sesame & white
    chocolate cupcakes
    107–8
blackberries: blackberry
    apple crumble
    cupcakes 104–6
blackberry
    buttercream 104–6
blondies: banana
    blondie 142
    raspberry white
        chocolate blondie 150
blow torches 14
blueberries: blueberry
    & yoghurt buttercreams
    95–6
    blueberry buttercream 36
    blueberry cheesecake
        254–6
    Swiss meringue
        buttercream 40
bonfire bar 163–4
bowls 12
breakfast bowl cupcakes
    95–6
brownies: C&D chocolate
    brownie 34
    caramel cornflake
        brownie 132
    cookie dough
        brownie 152
    Marathon brownie 144
    s'mores brownie 157–8
    triple decker
        brownie 138
burnt butter 56
    banana blondie 142
    burnt butter
        buttercream 122–4
    burnt butter sponge
        101–2
    cookie dough
        cake 257–8

raspberry white
    chocolate blondie 150
butter 16
    burnt butter 56
    softening 21
buttercream: basic
    buttercream 36
    Biscoff buttercream 194
    blackberry buttercream
        104–6
    blueberry & yoghurt
        buttercreams 95–6
    burnt butter
        buttercream 122–4
    cake balls 260
    cake batter
        buttercream 84
    cereal milk
        buttercream 74
    cinnamon buttercream
        98–100
    hazelnut buttercream 88
    hibiscus 113–14
    kirsch buttercream
        125–6
    miso caramel
        buttercream 92–4
    raspberry
        buttercream 82
    salted caramel
        buttercream 44,
        101–2
    Swiss meringue
        buttercream 40
    yuzu buttercream
        116–18
buttermilk: chocolate
    cupcakes 32
    chocolate sponge 30
    end of the world
        chocolate cake 218–20
    Ferrero Rocher cake
        236–8
    Marathon cake 251–2
    raspberry bombe
        cupcakes 82
    s'mores cake 230–2
    velvet volcano cake
        215–16

C

C&D chocolate
    brownie 34
cake balls 260
cake batter cupcakes 84
cake levellers 14
cake rings 14
cake scrapers 14
cake tins 12
cakes 209–61
    birthday cake 212–14
    chocolate sponge 30
    cookie dough cake
        257–8
    end of the world
        chocolate cake 218–20
    Ferrero Rocher cake
        236–8
    honey crunch nut cake
        227–8
    lemon mess cake 242–4
    Marathon cake 251–2
    matcha & black sesame
        cake 233–4
    raspberry & yuzu cake
        224–6
    raspberry, pistachio &
        chocolate cake 248–50
    salted caramel cake
        245–6
    s'mores cake 230–2
    sticky toffee cake 239–40
    tiramisu cake 221–2
    vanilla sponge 26
    velvet volcano cake
        215–16
    see also cupcakes;
        traybakes
candied black sesame
    seeds 107–8, 233–4
caramel: banana caramel
    122–4
    caramel apple
        cheesecake 146
    caramel cornflake
        brownie 132
    caramel pretzel cookie
        sarnies 196–8
    caramelised white
        chocolate 54

Index

cornflake caramel
132, 148
honey caramel 86
miso caramel cupcakes
92-4
miso caramel
buttercream 36
cherry buttercream 36
chewy choc chip
cookies 176
chocolate 18-19
apple crumble NY
cookies 192
banana blondie 142
birthday cake NY
cookies 184
Biscoff rocky road 136
Black Forest cupcakes
125-6
black ganache 92-4
black sesame & white
chocolate cupcakes
107-8
C&D chocolate
brownie 34
cake balls 260
caramel cornflake
brownie 132
caramel pretzel cookie
sarnies 196-8
caramelised white
chocolate 54
cereal fun bar 134
chewy choc chip
cookies 176
chocolate cream
cheese icing 38
chocolate cupcakes 32
chocolate ganache
drizzle 172
chocolate insanity
cupcakes 76
chocolate shards 218-20
chocolate sponge 30
chocolate truffles
218-20, 221-2
cookie cheesecake 140
cookie dough
brownie 152
cookie dough cake
257-8
cookie dough cookies
190
double choc NY
cookies 174
end of the world
chocolate cake 218-20

Ferrero Rocher cake
236-8
Ferrero Rocher
cupcakes 88
funfetti sponge 84
ganache 52, 148, 152,
157-8
ginger & Biscoff NY
cookies 188
mallow wheels 199-200
triple decker
brownie 138
milk chocolate ganache
138
Marathon brownie 144
Marathon cake 251-2
milk chocolate passion
fruit cupcakes 119-20
miso caramel cupcakes
92-4
pie crumb 64
pink chocolate drizzle
160-2
raspberry bombe
cupcakes 82
raspberry, pistachio &
chocolate cake 248-50
raspberry white
chocolate blondie 150
red velvet NY cookies 180
skillet cookie 186
s'mores brownie 157-8
s'mores cake 230-2
Swiss meringue
buttercream 40
tahini & chocolate
cupcakes 80
tempering 19
truffles 76
Twicks bites 202-4
vegan Biscoff sandwich
cookies 194
velvet volcano cake
215-16
walnut choc chip NY
cookies 170
white chocolate &
sesame decorations 92-4
white chocolate discs
224-6
cinnamon: cinnamon
buttercream 98-100
cinnamon pie crumb 64
cocoa powder 18
coconut: bonfire bar
163-4
coffee 18

chocolate cupcakes 32
chocolate mudcakes 76
chocolate sponge 30
end of the world
chocolate cake 218-20
espresso buttercream 36
Ferrero Rocher cake 236-8
Marathon cake 251-2
raspberry bombe
cupcakes 82
s'mores cake 230-2
tiramisu cake 221-2
colourings 18
French meringue
('poops') 46
containers 14
cookie cutters 14
cookies 167-207
apple crumble NY
cookies 192
birthday cake NY
cookies 184
Biscoff cookie cups 205-6
caramel pretzel cookie
sarnies 196-8
chewy choc chip
cookies 176
cookie cheesecake 140
cookie dough 66
cookie dough
brownie 152
cookie dough cake 257-8
cookie dough cookies 190
double choc NY
cookies 174
ginger & Biscoff NY
cookies 188
ginger creams 182
mallow wheels 199-200
PB&J sarnies 178
red velvet NY cookies 180
skillet cookie 186
Twicks bites 202-4
vegan Biscoff sandwich
cookies 194
velvet volcano cookie
cups 172
walnut choc chip NY
cookies 170
cooling racks 14
cornflakes: caramel
cornflake brownie 132
cereal milk cupcakes 74
malty cornflakes 68
OG cornflake crunch 148
peanut malty cornflakes
227-8

crackle cookies 196-8
cream 17
black ganache 92-4
chocolate ganache 52
chocolate ganache
drizzle 172
chocolate sauce filling 76
ganache 148, 152
milk chocolate
ganache 138
sticky toffee sauce
239-40
strawberry cream
filling 110-12
cream cheese: Biscoff
cookie cups 205-6
caramel apple
cheesecake 146
cookie cheesecake 140
cream cheese icing
38, 182
ginger cheesecake
163-4
strawberry shortcake
cheesecakes 160-2
crème mousseline 50
rhubarb & custard
cupcakes 78
crème pâtissière 50
crisps, apple 98-100
crumble pie crumb 64
crumble topping 146
cupcake tins 12
cupcakes 71-127
apple pie cupcakes
98-100
baklava cupcakes 86
bananarama cupcakes
122-4
Black Forest cupcakes
125-6
black sesame & white
chocolate cupcakes
107-8
blackberry apple
crumble cupcakes 104-6
breakfast bowl cupcakes
95-6
cake batter cupcakes 84
cereal milk cupcakes 74
chocolate cupcakes 32
chocolate insanity
cupcakes 76
Ferrero Rocher
cupcakes 88
hibiscus & lime cupcakes
113-14

Key lime pie cupcakes
90
milk chocolate passion
fruit cupcakes 119-20
miso caramel cupcakes
92-4
raspberry bombe
cupcakes 82
rhubarb & custard
cupcakes 78
roasted strawberry &
yuzu cupcakes 116-18
salted caramel pretzel
cupcakes 101-2
strawberry shortcake
cupcakes 110-12
tahini & chocolate
cupcakes 80
vanilla cupcakes 28
custard 50
rhubarb & custard
cupcakes 78

D
dates: sticky toffee cake
239-40
demerara sugar 16
digestive biscuits: Key
lime pie cupcakes 90
s'mores brownie 157-8
double choc NY
cookies 174

E
eggs 17
electric hand mixers 12
end of the world
chocolate cake 218-20
equipment 12-14
espresso buttercream 36
espresso sponge 221-2

F
Ferrero Rocher
cake 236-8
Ferrero Rocher
cupcakes 88
flour 17
food colouring 18
food processors 12
French meringue
('poops') 45-6
funfetti sponge 84

G
ganache 52, 148, 152, 157-8
black ganache 92-4
buttery ganache icing 52
chocolate ganache
drizzle 172
milk chocolate
ganache 138
ginger: bonfire bar 163-4
ginger & Biscoff NY
cookies 188
ginger creams 182
sticky toffee cake 239-40
glaze, hibiscus 113-14
gluten-free flour 17
golden syrup: syrup
sponge 98-100, 245-6
goo 60
granola topping 95-6,
104-6
graters 14
greaseproof paper 14

H
hazelnuts: Ferrero
Rocher cake 236-8
Ferrero Rocher
cupcakes 88
hazelnut buttercream
36, 88
hibiscus & lime cupcakes
113-14
hibiscus buttercream
113-14
Hobnobs: cookie
cheesecake 140
OG cornflake crunch 148
honey: honey caramel 86
honey crunch nut cake
227-8
Swiss meringue
buttercream 40
honeycomb, ginger 163-4

I
icing: buttery
ganache icing 52
cream cheese icing
38, 182
see also buttercream
icing sugar 16
ingredients 16-19
Italian meringue 48

J
jam: mallow wheels 199
PB&J sarnies 178

K
Key lime pie cupcakes 90
kirsch buttercream 125-6
knives 13

L
leftovers 21
cake balls 260
lemon: blueberry
cheesecake 254-6
lemon buttercream 36
lemon curd 58
lemon meringue bar
154-6
lemon mess cake 242-4
limes: hibiscus & lime
cupcakes 113-14
Key lime pie cupcakes 90
Lotus Biscoff spread see
Biscoff spread

M
mallow wheels 199-200
malted milk powder:
malty cornflakes 68
peanut malty cornflakes
227-8
Marathon brownie 144
Marathon cake 251-2
marshmallows: Biscoff
rocky road 136
cereal fun bar 134
mallow wheels 199-200
Marathon brownie 144
nougat 138
peanutty nougat 251-2
triple decker
brownie 138
mascarpone icing 38
matcha: matcha & black
sesame cake 233-4
pie crumb 64
Swiss meringue
buttercream 40
meringue: Ferrero
Rocher cake 236-8
French meringue
('poops') 45-6
Italian meringue 48
Key lime pie cupcakes 90
lemon meringue bar 154-6
lemon mess cake 242-4
rainbow poops 212-14
s'mores brownie 157-8
s'mores cake 230-2
strawberry shortcake
cheesecakes 160-2

meringue buttercream,
Swiss 40
microplane graters 14
milk 17
crème pâtissière 50
milk chocolate passion
fruit cupcakes 119-20
miso caramel cupcakes
92-4
mixed peel: ginger &
Biscoff NY cookies 188
mixers 12
mudcakes: chocolate 76
white chocolate 92-4,
107-8
muscovado sugar 16

N
nougat: Marathon
brownie 144
peanutty nougat 251-2
triple decker
brownie 138
nuts: nut butter 62
see also pecans,
walnuts etc
NY cookies: apple
crumble 192
birthday cake 184
double choc 174
ginger & Biscoff 188
red velvet 180
walnut choc chip 170

O
oats: crumble topping 146
granola topping 95-6,
104-6
OG cornflake crunch 148
Oreos: Oreo
buttercream 36
velvet volcano cake
215-16
oven gloves 13
oven thermometers 13
ovens 21

P
palette knives 14
paper cases 13
passion fruit: milk
chocolate passion fruit
cupcakes 119-20
peanut butter: honey
crunch nut cake 227-8
Marathon brownie 144
Marathon cake 251-2

PB&J sarnies 178
peanut butter
    buttercream 36
peanuts: Marathon
    brownie 144
    peanut malty cornflakes
    227-8
    peanutty nougat 251-2
pecans: banana
    blondie 142
    bonfire bar 163-4
pie crumb 64
pink chocolate drizzle
    160-2
piping bags 14
piping nozzles 14
pistachios: baklava
    cupcakes 86
    raspberry, pistachio &
    chocolate cake 248-50
    Swiss meringue
    buttercream 40
    poops 45-6
    Ferrero Rocher
    cake 236-8
    rainbow poops 212-14
pretzels: caramel pretzel
    cookie sarnies 196-8
    salted caramel pretzel
    cupcakes 101-2

R
rainbow poops 212-14
raising agents 17
raspberries: raspberry
    & yuzu cake 224-6
    raspberry bombe
    cupcakes 82
    raspberry buttercream
    36, 82
    raspberry, pistachio
    & chocolate cake
    248-50
    raspberry white
    chocolate blondie 150
    Swiss meringue
    buttercream 40
raspberry jam: PB&J
    sarnies 178
red velvet NY
    cookies 180
rhubarb & custard
    cupcakes 78
Rice Krispies: cereal
    fun bar 134
    triple decker
    brownie 138

rocky road, Biscoff 136
rolling pins 13

S
salt 17
    see also caramel
sandwich tins 12
saucepans 13
sauces: apple sauce 104-6
    apple sauce filling 98
    chocolate sauce
    filling 76
    sticky toffee sauce
    239-40
scales 12
scaling recipes up
    and down 21
seeds: granola topping
    95-6, 104-6
    sesame seeds: black
    sesame & white
    chocolate cupcakes
    107-8
    candied black sesame
    seeds 107-8, 233-4
    matcha & black sesame
    cake 233-4
    sesame brittle 80
    white chocolate &
    sesame decorations
    92-4
shortbread: lemon
    meringue bar 154-6
    strawberry shortcake
    cheesecakes 160-2
    strawberry shortcake
    cupcakes 110-12
    Twicks bites 202-4
sieves 13
skillet cookie 186
s'mores brownie 157-8
s'mores cake 230-2
soft brown sugar 16
spatulas 13
sponges: chocolate
    sponge 30
    removing from tins 21
    vanilla sponge 26
    see also cakes; cupcakes
spoon measures 12
spoons 13
stand mixers 12
sticky toffee
    cake 239-40
strawberries: roasted
    strawberry & yuzu
    cupcakes 116-18

strawberry
    buttercream 36
    strawberry shortcake
    cheesecakes 160-2
    strawberry shortcake
    cupcakes 110-12
Swiss meringue
    buttercream 40
sugar 16
sugar thermometers 13
Swiss meringue
    buttercream 40
    black sesame 107-8
    tahini & chocolate 80
    syrup sponge 98-100,
    245-6

T
tahini & chocolate
    cupcakes 80
tea: smoky caramel 163-4
    see also matcha powder
tempering chocolate 19
thermometers 13
timers 13
tins 12
removing sponges 21
tiramisu cake 221-2
traybakes 129-65
    banana blondie 142
    Biscoff rocky road 136
    bonfire bar 163-4
    C&D chocolate
    brownie 34
    caramel apple
    cheesecake 146
    caramel cornflake
    brownie 132
    cereal fun bar 134
    cookie cheesecake 140
    cookie dough
    brownie 152
    lemon meringue bar
    154-6
    Marathon brownie 144
    OG cornflake crunch 148
    raspberry white
    chocolate blondie 150
    s'mores brownie 157-8
    strawberry shortcake
    cheesecakes 160-2
triple decker
    brownie 138
truffles, chocolate 76,
    218-20, 221-2
turntables 14
Twicks bites 202-4

V
vanilla 18
    basic buttercream 36
    vanilla cupcakes 28
    vanilla funfetti sponge
    212-14
    vanilla sponge 26
vegan recipes: raspberry,
    pistachio & chocolate
    cake 248-50
    vegan Biscoff sandwich
    cookies 194
    velvet volcano cake
    215-16
    velvet volcano cookie
    cups 172

W
walnut choc chip NY
    cookies 170
whisks 13
white chocolate 19
    apple crumble NY
    cookies 192
    birthday cake NY
    cookies 184
    Biscoff rocky road 136
    black sesame & white
    chocolate cupcakes
    107-8
    caramelised white
    chocolate 54
    cereal fun bar 134
    ginger & Biscoff NY
    cookies 188
    miso caramel cupcakes
    92-4
    pink chocolate drizzle
    160-2
    raspberry white
    chocolate blondie 150
    red velvet NY cookies 180
    white chocolate & sesame
    decorations 92-4
    white chocolate discs
    224-6
    white chocolate ganache 52
wooden spoons 13

Y
yoghurt: breakfast bowl
    cupcakes 95-6
yuzu juice: raspberry
    & yuzu cake 224-6
yuzu buttercream
    36, 116-18

PENGUIN MICHAEL JOSEPH

UK | USA | Canada | Ireland | Australia
India | New Zealand | South Africa

Penguin Michael Joseph is part of the Penguin Random House group of
companies whose addresses can be found at global.penguinrandomhouse.com

First published 2022
001

Set in Shorai and Alright Sans
Design by Studio Polka
Props and art direction by Daisy Shayler-Webb
Food styling by Team Cupcake Jemma and Crumbs & Doilies
Colour reproduction by Altaimage Ltd
Printed in Italy by Elcograf S.p.A

The authorized representative in the EEA is Penguin Random House Ireland,
Morrison Chambers, 32 Nassau Street, Dublin D02 YH68

A CIP catalogue record for this book is available from the British Library

isbn: 978-0-241-61084-8

www.greenpenguin.co.uk